# STORES
## OF THE YEAR

No. 15

Carlos Miele

# STORES
## OF THE YEAR

## No. 15

**Martin M. Pegler**

VISUAL REFERENCE PUBLICATIONS, INC., New York, NY

Visual Reference Publications, Inc.
302 Fifth Avenue
New York, NY 10001

Distributors to the trade in the United States and Canada
Watson-Guptill
770 Broadway
New York, NY  10003

Distributors outside the United States and Canada
HarperCollins International
10 E. 53rd Street
New York, NY  10022

Library of Congress Cataloging in Publication Data:
Stores of the Year 15

Printed in China
ISBN 1-58471-088-8

Book Design: Judy Shepard

Steve Madden

# TABLE OF CONTENTS

Holt Renfrew

# INTRODUCTION

With each succeeding edition of Stores of the Year, we realize and prove that Retail Design has been internationalized. When the first few editions were published we were an island unto ourselves and showed only U.S. projects designed by U.S. designers for the U.S. market. Things have changed! The retail design scene has changed and international barriers—no matter how invisible—have melted away and the whole world is looking at and reacting to new designs almost at the same time. Noted architects/designers from The Netherlands, France and Italy are creating boutiques and shops on Madison Avenue and Soho in New York City just as there are Italian and U.S. designers coming up with eye-popping retail wonders in Tokyo. An American designer working in Milan has designed a boutique in Moscow! U.S. designers are extending their know-how in merchandise presentation and promotion around the world—literally—as they build top notch department stores in Russia, Korea, Mexico and Chile—to name only a few locations.

For this edition, we have stepped back only so that we can step forward, and we are showing some of the recent department stores built in the U.S. as well as around the world. While we in the U.S. are asking the same tired question—"Are department stores dying or are they already dead?"—in developing areas around the world they are just discovering the wonders of the department store as a viable all-in-one shopping experience. From the department stores and their shops-within-the-shop come design concepts that are relevant to other more focused retail store designs In addition we have included new retail chains as well as prototype designs created for established retailers who are looking for new and younger target markets. The premise, as the reader will see visually throughout this edition, is to gain a new and memorable look without losing the good will and continued patronage of the customer base. The world is changing, the consumer is changing and the retail design must keep up with—and get a few steps ahead of—this ever-changing audience.

No Stores of the Year book would be complete without some designer boutiques because from their usual minimalist approach we can learn something that can be applied to upscaling or up-marketing a retail image. So as not to appear snobbish or elitist, we have included some excellent examples of more middle-of-the-road or popular-priced merchandise can be housed and presented with style and a degree of sophistication.

Many of the 50 projects included in this volume that have been selected from around the world are fashion oriented, but there is a growing trend towards creating fashionable settings for hard goods as well as the soft. The whole communications area has grown in the last few years and so we have included some of the fabulous retail stores that have been designed to house electronic and computer products.

Stores of the Year 15 is only a sampling of the ever-growing, ever-expanding and ever-evolving retail design field. As I travel internationally I am seeing more and more exciting store designs in places where they never existed before. I am finding more and more fresh, young and creative talent sprouting up in places where a store was once no more than a glorified warehouse or an indoor bazaar. I am looking forward to Stores of the Year 16 at which time I hope to introduce the readers to the expanding list of international designers, including those emerging in India, China and some of the awakening South American countries.

Please stay tuned for future developments.

Martin M. Pegler

# TSUM

Moscow, Russia

DESIGN: **Point Design,** New York, NY
**Diego Garay**

Tsum, Moscow's "original and only true department store," has recently been renovated and revived to match the young Russian population that has been rapidly moving from "communism to consumerism." The historic—more then a century old—Belle Epoque building is beautifully located in central Moscow. It is situated near the tourist-ridden Red Square and the dance Mecca—the Bolshoi Theater.

The original store opened in 1890 and at that time featured quality, selection, exclusive and original products, innovation as a retailer—and service. Under the Communist Regime (1917-1992) it remained a destination for those who could afford to shop there though the merchandise and the presentation was old-fashioned, predictable, unimagi-

native and often disorganized. In 2003 it was taken over by Moscow's Mercury Group. This organization has been successfully introducing trendsetting fashions and luxury goods from top designers and brand names such as Armani, Prada and Ferrari. They are now turning Tsum into what they hope will be "Europe's most beautiful, large-scale retail venue." To carry out their vision they called upon the talents of Diego Garay and his company, Point Design of New York. Point Design was selected to renovate the store in a series of phases because, as Alexander Rebok, Tsum's general manager said, "They bring a wealth of retail experience combined with a high degree of creativity and resourcefulness."

Diego Garay says, "There has never been a better time to be a retailer in Russia. Over the last decade, there has been a rapid switch from communism to consumerism. The growing number of 'newly rich' young Russians has been persuaded to believe that money is best spent on tangible things. Mercury Group was among the first to realize that

Moscow needed a glamorous new place to shop and believes Tsum will be the exciting solution."

Today, the 360,000 sq. ft. store features high-end fashions and luxury goods and top international designers such as Chanel, Prada and Armani. Using a sophisticated palette that incorporates polished and honed stones, mosaic tiles, textured wall coverings and dramatic lighting, "the store takes on an entirely fresh and elegant approach to a tried and proven format." The layout is fairly traditional: Cosmetics and Fashion Accessories on the main level, Menswear on two, Women's Wear on three, Young Fashions on four and Housewares on five. According to Diego Garay, "Throughout, spaces

flow easily from one to the other, and nowhere does the environment compete with the merchandise. In fact, color, lighting, featuring and special arrangements all work together to present what's offered with drama and clarity." The design on the dynamic central atrium not only sets the look for the new Tsum but also serves as a gathering place for events and showcasing special products. Garay says that this "treatment of both public space and merchandising is new to Moscow."

The success of this new renovated store has the Mercury Group planning to double the size of this Moscow store in the very near future and they are looking to expand into St. Petersburg—and other major cities in Russia.

# HOUSE OF FRASER

The City, London, UK

Strange as it may seem—but true—The House of Fraser, located in what was originally the Guardian Royal Exchange Banking Hall, is the first department store to open its doors in The City of London in over 30 years. It was worth waiting for! This new flagship store for the chain occupies five floors and 40,000 sq. ft. of space and boasts an all-new interior and graphics designed by KKD. "It is smaller than other stores in the House of Fraser group and consequently the range of product is highly selective and in keeping with the affluence and aspirations of the City customer. The store presents a single and unified identity, offering a boutique style format to showcase capsule collections of leading brands and exclusive designer labels."

For those unfamiliar with London, The City refers to the area adjacent to the River Thames and the South Bank. It is the heart of the commercial and banking area and this store is around the corner from the giant memorial column that commemorates the great fire of 1666 when most of this area was totally razed and then rebuilt with many Christopher Wren edifices. According to the designers, "The interplay between the old and new sees the Edwardian façade projecting grandeur and an expectation of luxury contrasting with the glamorous modern interior. Simple light forms, using stone, glass, mirror and walnut, convey a sleek, contemporary and luxury edge." The new escalator well, in the center of the space, encourages circulation between the floors.

Menswear is located below ground level while cosmetics takes up most of the airy, daylight-filled, high-ceilinged ground level. Premium gifts and luxury giftware share the first

DESIGN: KKD: **Kinnersley Kent Design,** London
PHOTOGRAPHY: **Carlos Dominguez**

level with premium accessories. Young Fashions are on the second floor and the third level is devoted to Designer Fashions and Lingerie. Throughout, the building's grid of columns has been wrapped with mirrors and illuminated panels of glass "to maximize the feeling of light and space." Since the original steel windows of the building have been retained, the interior of the store is literally flooded with natural light from the south façade.

Each floor has a different finish "to create subtle shifts in mood": green-blue sandstone for the floors in men's, white floor tiles in cosmetics and limestone in accessories and

designer womenswear. In contemporary womenswear gray ceramic tiles were laid. Though essentially white throughout the store (walls and ceilings), the designers have designated a key color in simple, chunky acrylic blocks along with specific graphics to delineate the floors: red for menswear, pink for cosmetics, champagne on accessories and gifts, orange for the contemporary level and pale green for designer and lingerie. "This color scheme is carried through to the display trays, store directories, mannequins, photographic imagery and visual elements—creating a strong, coherent language." KKD also developed a

new merchandising system of flexible, hanging/shelving made of stainless steel and glass that allows the back walls to "remain completely clean—giving a real feeling of lightness and luxury."

It really was worth waiting 30 years for a store like this. It gives additional meaning to the word "luxurious" and it is a delight to shop.

# HARVEY NICHOLS

Manchester, UK

DESIGN: **FOUR IV,** London, UK
CREATIVE DIRECTOR: **Chris Dewar Dixon**
INTERIORS: **Michele Barker, Ben Murphy**
GRAPHICS: **Richard Clayton**
PROJECT MANAGER: **Louise Barnard**
PHOTOGRAPHY: **Richard Clayton, James Windspear**

The fifth store in the Harvey Nichols chain of upscale specialty stores opened in The Shambles in Manchester in the UK. The 60,000 sq. ft. department store is set out on three levels and as the designers of the store, FOUR IV, say, "Harvey Nichols brings world class shopping to the North's best dressed and most discerning." In this store, using elegant and exquisite materials, the design "expresses a united Harvey Nichols design concept that evolves in texture and color from department to department—floor to floor."

There is a feeling of openness and transparency throughout the space. The building's architecture expresses Art Deco motifs and it has a curved tower that rises up—filled with curved, draped and illuminated windows that serve as "a nighttime beacon." Sheer drapery featured else-where in the store "subtly divide departments and encourage a member's club atmosphere and a heightened sense of being on the inside." The shopper enters through a double height, fully-glazed entrance into the fashionable store. Cream is the major color of the palette for this floor and it is complemented by a deep peat dark brown. The design team allowed the materials and highlighting colors to evolve as the shopper moves through the space and the furniture and fixtures that were selected are "key to fostering an intimacy in a big store." Chunky framed mirrors and floor standing lights with cream colored fabric shades "steer the eye."

In keeping with the luxury attitude of HN—never one to encourage skimping on life's sparkling essentials—the jewelry department is up front and includes special collections by the Crown jeweler, Garrard, and the society jewelry designer Theo Fennell. Adjacent is leather goods and a display of the season's "must-have" handbags. Very HN and very Hollywood Glamour is the sweeping black and gold granite staircase ahead that is set off by the gold-colored walls. Along the way the shopper can linger in the cosmetics area with its relief wallpaper and custom sand-blasted acrylic panels. The impression here is of "a forest dappled light." Long, oblong box lighting with chandeliers printed on the surface hang over the equally long cosmetics tables. The fragrance samplers are individually recessed in a fixture of interlocking, illuminated Perspex fins set along an illuminated wall of white translucent panels. Conical drums rise up from the floor—in the center of the space—to display the fragrance

products. Also on this level the shopper may opt for having her teeth whitened, maybe a Botox stop or sip some juice at the juice bar set within a colored glass walled area. Visible throughout this level is a dramatic black lacquer and gold hatched wall that rises up through the floors of the escalator void.

Pink is the reigning color on the first level where women's wear is presented. The name brand areas are separated by sheer pink fabric screens that are flecked with gold. Further creating a feeling of intimacy are the pink fabric light shades that cast a soft, warm, glowing light. The cash desk, here, is inlaid with a specially-designed decorative aluminum film.

Men's wear is on the second floor and here the colors are darker and "more masculine" with dark oak floors and amber honeycombed, Perspex screens. These "add texture

and mood to the environment." The garments are presented in massive wardrobes that also serve to divide the space into branded areas. A black granite and marble restaurant is also located on this level.

Gregor Jackson, design director of Four IV said, "The quality of materials HN has invested in is opulent and confirms its self-belief as the world's finest department store retailer, and in its new customers in Manchester as deserving the best. We feel that we have captured the essence of Harvey Nichols and expressed it into this new store via every conceivable detail and innovation."

# NORDSTROM

Fashion Show, Las Vegas, NV

DESIGN: **Callison Architects,** Seattle, WA
PHOTOGRAPHY: **Chris Eden,** Seattle, WA

Las Vegas is pure theater and to make its appearance in the new, three-level, 200,000 sq. ft. store on the glittering and sparkling Las Vegas Boulevard, Nordstrom pulled out all the stops. In a world going giddy and glitzy, Callison Architects of Seattle created a real, high-class oasis in the midst of the furor going on all around. "The designers focused on creating an understated, timeless architecture reminiscent of the arrival experience at a quality resort. From its prominent porte cochere entrance and lush landscaping to the distinctive lifestyle merchandising

inside, Nordstrom Las Vegas presents a thoroughly inviting experience."

Visitors as well as locals are invited to step in from the strong desert sunlight under the arched, cantilevered canopy that extends out from the gridded, contemporary facade. The interior follows through the "customer-friendly" feeling by presenting the merchandise in lifestyle storytelling in approachable and accessible ways. A light ash backwall is common to each floor and holds the store together. The individual casework and custom fixtures "support the focus on merchandise vignettes that explain fashion statements and show coordinating items." A vaulted ceiling runs the length of the first floor and it connects "the drama and elegance of the valet entrance" (the porte cochere) to the mall entrance into the store. Here, a warm palette of sandstone and wood make a quiet contrast to the high-tech shine and glitter of the revamped Fashion Show shopping center.

The ground level of the store is full of interactive experiences for the shopper. It is the World of Make-Up and Fragrance; it is where there are opportunities to sample and for

demonstrations to observe or partici-
pate in. A Nail Bar and Candle Bar
are only two of the unique shops
within the shop. To make the large
cosmetic department even more customer friendly, the designers introduced a "topography of varying
heights" and display "pods" that can
be converted to many different uses.

The second level is the Women's
World and it was designed to accom-
modate the varied lifestyles and tastes
of Nordstrom shoppers. Savvy, Col-
lectors, via C, and TBD are each
defined by their customized decor
and fixtures and a visual presentation
and merchandising system that is
unique to each separate boutique.
Shoppers can readily identify what
appeals to them.

Throughout, the classic taste and
sophistication of the Nordstrom
organization is evident in the design
and look of the store. This store also
recognizes and acknowledges the
potential market of "high-rolling"
visitors to gaudy, naughty Las Vegas
and provides them with the Nordstrom experience that they would
expect with amenities such as a café,
a concierge, personal shoppers and
valet parking.

# HOLT RENFREW—MAIN FLOOR

Toronto, ON, Canada

The award winning renovation of Holt Renfrew's flagship store in Toronto is the work of the Burdifilek design firm. The challenge was to "translate the Holt Renfrew brand into a physical environment" and to do that the designers adopted an understanding of that brand, its reputation as a leader in high-end Canadian retailing and the clientele that Holt Renfrew caters to. "Understanding a client's brand is not only important, it's paramount. Retail design for a luxury store is a complex process. We needed to create an atmosphere that was an extension of Holt Renfrew's personality, prestige, and that embodied the essence of their iconic and design-driven history."

The result, as illustrated on these pages, is firmly rooted in "the realm of sophisticated modernism." Using exotic woods, a sensitive color palette and custom finishes and artwork along with compartmentalized departments and exciting site lines, the designers created "a unique sensory experience that is distinctly Holt Renfrew." Cosmetics, fine jewelry, soft accessories, handbags and the men's department share the newly-renovated main floor of the store. Burdifilek created an "umbrella" or single unifying look for the floor and then customized each area with "sensitive architectural details." A choice collection of

DESIGN: **Burdifilek,** Toronto, ON
PRINCIPALS: **Diego Burdi, Paul Filek**

high-end companies are represented in the cosmetics/toiletries area and each is defined with consistent finishes, textures and customized millwork—a first in the Canadian retail marketplace.

A "sense of grandeur" is immediately apparent in the fine jewelry department where the collections are displayed "poetically under starfire glass on museum cases." The background combines custom birch bark and alabaster finishes. Handbags are set out on shelves floating off pale gray walls and on tables, pedestals and chests of the same fine, sophisticated look. The totally neutral color scheme makes each bag appear as a work of art to be studied and appreciated in the round —like a piece of sculpture. The soft, targeted light enhances the overall ambiance and highlights the featured bags.

The men's department follows.

DESIGN: **Burdifilek,** Toronto ON
PRINCIPALS: **Diego Burdi, Paul Filek**

The men's department, also on the main level of the renovated Holt Renfrew flagship store in Toronto, follows through on the store design concept previously shown. Burdifilek, the designers, created a feeling of "individuality, beauty and luxury in the retail environment."

This area is distinguished by having the classic contemporary collection of men's designer and top name brands shown against sculptural imbuya wood and on stone and Lucite display tables.

# LIVERPOOL

Galerias Guadalajara, Guadalajara, Mexico

DESIGN: **RYA, Retail Designers & Consultants,**
Dallas, TX
DESIGN TEAM
RYA ASSOCIATE PRINCIPAL: **Robert Coker**
SR. ASSOCIATE: **Jeff Henderson**
ARCHITECTURE: **Luis Olecea, El Puerto de
Liverpool,** Mexico City, Mexico
GRAPHICS: **Rocio Martinex,** Mexico City, Mexico
PHOTOGRAPHY: **Andrea Brizzi,** New York, NY

Guadalajara is the second largest city in Mexico—after Mexico City—and where the newest addition to the El Puerto de Liverpool department stores recently opened in the equally new and strikingly handsome Galerias Guadalajara. The mall, located amid other malls in a high-density retail area of the city, is the major attraction for the five million residents of Greater Guadalajara.

According to Robert Coker, Associate Principal of RYA of Dallas, the designers of the almost 300,000 sq. ft. space, "The design is rooted in the Modernist idiom." The design relies on an interplay of form, color, light and texture to create a selling environment that is welcoming and accessible to its customers." In keeping with the store's design is the bold and dynamic use of color in identification, branding and merchandising. "Throughout every aspect of the store environment color accentuates, enlivens and identifies individual 'rooms' for visualization of the individual departments and promotional private brands."

The dominant design theme—and color—is established in the central atrium of the store with the crimson ("crimson signifies transportation") escalator that is the focal point in the dramatic, open space. "The boldly-colored epicenter of the store serves as an icon for Liverpool's new and youthful image." Throughout the three levels the design team used bright, strong colors to create vivid focal highlights on the high perimeter walls and the lower interior ones. Color is also used to "sculpturally enhance the architecture."

Light plays a vital role—along with color—in affecting the bright, lively feeling that permeates the spacious store. Natural light streams in through the deeply shaded clerestory of the central atrium and internally-illuminated, translucent glass columns serve as dynamic backgrounds for centrally located shops. Adding to the natural light from the atrium, each of the major axes terminate at an exterior wall with glazed openings. "The exterior light contribution is balanced by non-traditional light sources within the ceiling architecture to maintain the perception of overall brightness." An "avenue of light" is created by the previously mentioned illuminated columns that line the primary axis and terminate in shallow recesses lighted from concealed sources. Round, shallow recesses on the second level and rectangular ones on the first and third levels use asymmetrical light slots to highlight the mini-shops on the main aisles.

In contrast to the rectilinear organization of the floor plan there are

occasional curves and sweeps "to create an unexpected effect" such as the shallow serpentine curves of the aisle patterns that "entice customers to explore the length of the store." Large visual display/promotional presentation areas appear throughout. Circular cut-outs between the second and third levels also create a

sense of visual excitement as well as visually connecting the two floors. "These penetrations are aligned so that the customer senses the organization of the store and its family of business."

"Color, light and texture are key components in the composition of the store. All three components are

integral to the success of the design. However, it is clear that Liverpool Guadalajara is unafraid of color and is a testament to its value within the modern retail environment." This store's design was recognized and honored with awards from the SADI and the NASFM.

# LOTTE

Daegu Station, Daegu, South Korea

BIG!! Is about the best—and only— way to describe the new Lotte Department store in Daegu. This is the latest "jewel" in the crown that Lotte wears as South Korea's leading retailer, and the 12-level, 750,000-square-foot store is located in one of Korea's leading growth cities. This exciting structure—full of curves, arcs and contrasting planes—is located over a major subway station and the architectural design includes a pedestrian plaza, an attached five-level parking lot and two-level direct accesses to the subway station.

FRCH Design Worldwide was commissioned to design the retail spaces from Basement Level 2, up to Level 8. Their work included the architectural design, store planning, interior design, visual merchandising concepts and the lighting programs. This is a new look for Lotte: far more elegant than the stores that preceded this one. "The crisp interiors create a fresh contemporary background for Lotte's extensive merchandise collection and provides a destination for a full day of shopping that includes a youth zone, an international fresh food market and food court, restaurants, spas and movie theaters."

FRCH created an overall unifying concept "which allowed the flexibility to meet the store's diverse customer profile while maintaining a consistent

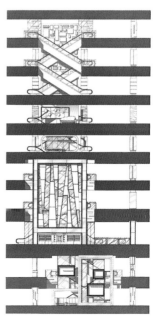

DESIGN: **FRCH Design Worldwide,** Cincinnati, OH
PHOTOGRAPHY: **Courtesy of FRCH**

Lotte Daegu Station store." The concept that was devised was "Lotte as a Jewel Box," with each level represented by a different gem color and pattern. This concept enabled the design to flow and adjust freely from floor to floor, while re-introducing and repeating common themes:

- The finish on the Jewel Box is structured on the architecture.
- The pattern of the Jewel Box is broadcast as the floor patterns.
- The style of the jewelry is projected as the pattern of the lighting.
- The metal of the setting is the binding accents in the details.
- The lining of the Jewel Box is the upholstery of the seating.
- The gemstone can be seen as the soft lighting peaking through the lid of the box."

This theme is reinforced in all the common areas within the store and by introducing the faceted gem patterns on the mostly marble floors. The round elevator lobbies "culminate as the Jewel Box with a cylindrical Jewel Box icon that highlights the premier merchandise and vendor on that floor." The escalator wells are the mode for transition from floor to floor within the Lotte Jewel Box design, where all the gemstones are alluded to within opalescent facets in platinum settings.

Basement Levels 4 and 3 are for parking, while the Celadon Level (B2) is a supermarket with marble floors and islands of products and services. These "create a marketplace style of merchandising." Amber is the gemstone of level B1, where shoppers can enter directly from the subway station. Here they will find import shops, footwear and leather goods. Woven leather perimeter frames and backlit, white, high-gloss painted platforms "create a masculine slab language for the light-filled shoe displays" in the 10,000-square-foot area.

Import boutiques and cosmetics are located on the first level—which is Topaz. This is the main entrance level and it features a three-level atrium and the hub for the vertical transportation in the store. The escalator is surrounded by

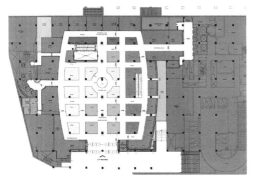

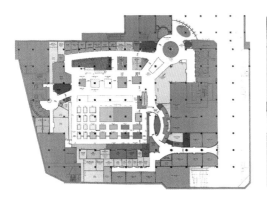

marble and the well is "draped by a dramatic art-glass wall of opalescent and transparent panels that are framed by masculine architectural frames—reflecting the modern Jewel Box."

Watches are shown in an island capped by a silver-leaf dome and surrounded by gem-patterned marble flooring. The column that seems to disappear into the ceiling adds a sense of height. The circular ceiling—a "feminine" design element— "serves as a strong visual point of reference and wayfinding for customers."

The Youth Zone on Level 4—Tur-

quoise—is a special area for teens and twenties and here the flooring is porcelain tile. Again the circular design elements appear and they are the visual icons of the building. Announcing the entry to the Youth Zone is the graphic icon column with floating stainless steel frames and blue neon trim. This floor is totally devoted to "trend-setting, fashion-forward young men and women." The latest fashions are presented on aisle-facing focal walls with back-painted glass panels. White lacquered columns with stainless steel overlay and curved soffits serve to

which is the children's and sports level. The sexes in the children's area are divided by a main aisle. On the 6th level—Tiger's Eye—is the 40,000-square-foot menswear area. Leather-wrapped column panels with gold, back-painted capitals, and bronze-framed and back-painted panels act as distinctive light troughs. "The balance of masculine lines with feminine surfaces defines the flexible styles of the Jewel Box."

The Food Court, consisting of vendor shops and restaurant chains as well as a coffee shop with wooden ceiling rings (an oasis for the shopper), is on the 8th level—Indigo. The designer boutiques are on 2 (Peridot) and women's is on 3 (Amethyst). Level 7—Emerald—is turned over to home and electronics. The movie theaters are on 9 and 10.

This store opened to a $4.5 million first day! Obviously, Daegu was ready and waiting for the Lotte Jewel Box—and the shoppers were not disappointed. Soon another Lotte (Sang-In) will open, also in Daegu City.

direct traffic through the floor. Throughout the store, all of the icon graphic signage "evokes a sense of international airports and travel."

Plastic laminate, color-coded checkerboard columns and vinyl tile flooring distinguish the Ruby floor—Level 5—

# SELFRIDGES KIDS

Oxford St., London, UK

Vittorio Raddice, the CEO of the world famous Selfridges Department Stores has been working hard at changing the store's image. He, his staff and the design firms he has been commissioning have been turning "the comfortable old cardie (cardigan sweater or button-up) into the Sexy Giant." Much has been noted about the revolutionary designs in the Manchester Store in Trafford Centre and now the "revolution" follows through on Oxford Street in the London Flagship store.

Future Systems working with Umdasch Shop Concepts, the noted designer/manufacturer of fittings and systems, have recently refitted and drastically changed the look of the 1,500 sq. meter (15,840 sq. ft) children's department. The area is now filled with soft lines and rounded forms made of deep drawn plastic. "The organically-inspired soft lines and forms are a central theme of Selfridges' children's department" and the uniqueness of the design was rewarded by being selected as the winner of "the outstanding retail experience award" by the prestigious British trade magazine, *Retail Interiors.* For children and their parents the new department is an adventure—almost like being Alice in Wonderland—on a different planet. This is actually "wander-land" since the traditional traffic patterns do not exist here and shoppers meander in and around the non-directional forms and they "find" things along the way. The fixtures/floor fittings are all white, bulbous shapes: some are low and squat with interior shelf space and a flat display surface (or seat) on top while others are suspended from the low ceiling and thus are somewhat swayable. They are half shields with the clothes semi-enclosed within the plastic form. Most of the selling floor is covered with a vivid blue carpet bordered in shades of blue and

DESIGN: **Future Systems,** London, UK
HEAD OF DESIGN TEAM: **Harvinda**
CEO OF SELFRIDGES (at that time): **Vittorio Raddice**
FIXTURES/FITTINGS: **Umdasch Shop Concepts**
GENERAL CONTRACTOR: **Withey Contracts**
PHOTOGRAPHY: **Courtesy of Umdasch**

finished off with a brilliant red orange.
A red accent color appears as a fascia
over the perimeter held garments. The
on-the-floor structural columns are
sheathed in a deep, dark blue plastic
mirror-like material that adds to the
spaceship fantasy setting and that
outer space feeling is further enhanced
by the eerie blue light emanating from
above the fascia and thus tinting the
white ceiling.

The snaking, curving and undulat-
ing lines of the fixtures are echoed on
some of the perimeter walls as well.
The shoe department curves around
itself and the white plastic "boulders"
provide unusual seating and some
serve as on-the-floor displayers. That
same serpentine wall treatment is evident in the Baby Gift area and in the
Toy space adjacent. In the Toy area
there are bulbous, bright orange
"seats" that also serve as kneeling
pads for children who want to watch
the raised train do its thing. In addition, on an amoeba shaped, orange
rug there is a play area where children can sit on sausage-shaped bean

bags and examine the available games
and books.

This giant floor is divided up into
seven concept areas which in addition
to shoes and baby gifts and, of course,
clothes for boys and girls and different age clusters, includes a "kid's
supermarket" where youngsters can
buy candies and play games. This
really is WONDERLAND.

# SEARS GRAND

W. Jordan, UT

DESIGN: **Pavlik Design Team,** Ft. Lauderdale, FL
PRESIDENT/CEO: **RJ Pavlik**
DIRECTOR OF PROJECTS: **Armando Castillo**
CREATIVE DIRECTOR: **Sherif Ayad**
DESIGN ADMINISTRATIVE DIRECTOR: **Placido Herrera**
PROJECT MANAGERS: **Amy Neumann,
Diane Santiago**
PROJECT DESIGNER: **Wendy Wright**
ASST. PROJECT DESIGNER: **Tiera Lindsey**
LIGHTING DESIGNER: **Amy Ann S. Ehmcke**
GRAPHIC DESIGNER: **Ximena Navarette,
Jennifer Veltre**

For Sears:
VP OF FACILITIES PLANNING & CONSTRUCTION:
**Fred Rosenberg**
VP, STORE PLANNING: **David Rich**
VP, CONSTRUCTION: **Russell Arnold**
VP VM/IN-STORE MARKETING: **Rosemary Kastrava**
SVP, OFF THE MALL STRATEGY: **Jerry Post**
VP/GMM, OFF THE MALL STORES: **Teresa Boyd**

With over 25 years of experience as a retail store designer—nine of those with the Pavlik Design Team—Sherif Ayad very comfortably fills the position of Creative Director at that noted Ft. Lauderdale design firm. During that time he has added his knowledge and taste to the overall retail strategy and design direction of that firm and to all aspects of their design process.

As Creative Director of the Sears Grand store he and his team created the prototype for the new retail format and brand identity of that operation and it seemed only logical to turn to him for more information on the project shown here.

**MARTIN M. PEGLER: Thank you for taking time out to discuss Pavlik**

Design Team's Sears Grand project. From the images I have seen it certainly looks "grand" in the sense that "grand" means "big." So, some basics: How big is this operation and what is the "grand" in Sears Grand?

SHERIF AYAD: The name Sears Grand was introduced to differentiate this store format from the regular Sears stores while referring to its size and product offerings.

MMP: What was the original challenge presented to Pavlik? What did Sears want to accomplish and how did you go about satisfying their requirements?

SA: The challenge was to develop /design a 200,000 sq. ft.t store with a unique and casual image (value oriented) that offers consumers a wide assortment of goods. Sears Grand offers goods ranging from Dockers pants and Sony plasmas to milk and Kellogg's Corn Flakes.

This is not a department store, not a discount store, not a warehouse store; in fact, it's not even a Sears store as customers know it today. I believe that is what makes this store model a successful one…it has created a new niche in a very competitive market place.

MMP: How much of the original brief had to do with projecting the Sears retail brand image? How did you tackle that and how did you go out to reach the Sears customer?

SA: We wanted to maintain the Sears brand strengths throughout the store experience with a sense of renewal and revitalization of what Sears used to represent in American society generations ago. The new image and signal of renewal starts from the exterior to create a curiosity. The styling of the exterior is intended to be eye catching, attract female shoppers as well as men, and be contemporary and timeless.

MMP: In looking through these

Work. Play. And everything in between.

images of the store there are numerous nationally advertised brands represented along with Sear's in-house brands. Reebok, adidas, Panasonic, Samsung, Hitachi, Arrow, Dockers—they are all there but the over-riding emphasis seems to be the Sears brand name—and price. Is that the intention?

SA: Few, if any, retailers can boast as many national brands in as many product categories. The idea was to strategically present all of these brands under the Sears Grand umbrella.

**MMP: Would it be wrong to classify this store—architecturally—as a "big box" store even though there is the nicety of large areas of fenestration at either end of the store? In a store of this size what was the basic layout and traffic patterns Pavlik designed for Sears Grand?**

SA: I would not simply classify this store as a "big box" since it is "designed from the inside out" in the true sense of that expression. The store was literally shaped around the interior customer experience, flow of

merchandise, site lines, walking distances, and convenience.

**MMP: Obviously, in a store of this size and with as many departments—signage plays a vital role. Tell me about the departmental and directional signage systems and how photographic images were used to create a more shop-able space.**

SA: The signage system is really

divided into four categories:
1. Way finding: directional and departmental signage (as executed on the column enclosures).
2. Lifestyle: inspirational lifestyle images and key words that provoke an emotional relationship to the product offerings (as executed on the perimeter focal walls).
3. Brands: neutral colored brands are consistently featured throughout the

with overhead prosceniums (stage frame like structures). This provides a sense of architecture within this open environment.

• The overall footprint is divided into quadrants, each one being anchored by a pavilion housing fitting rooms.

**MMP: What about your color palette?**

SA: The overall palette is actually very neutral (white and gray) allowing a lot of opportunities to introduce vibrant departmental accent colors.

store at perimeters, slab wall, and pavilion walls.

4. Informational: price and product features at the product level.

**MMP: How did you visually divide the hard goods from the soft goods in this store? How did you make it easy for a shopper to find what he or she wants?**

SA: In such a large store, ease of shopping becomes a critical issue:

• There are two entrances (his and hers) with one leading into Women's Apparel and Home Fashions, and the other leading into Men's Apparel and Home Improvements.

• Hard lines (higher presentations) are around the perimeter while Soft lines (lower presentations) are on the central pads…resulting in open vistas and clear site lines across the space.

• A central merchandised boulevard divides the store and is articulated

**MMP: It seems that you employed halide down lights throughout for ambient lighting—which is quite bright. What did you do to soften or accentuate the fashion presentations?**

SA: We did use the halides for ambient lighting while accent lighting was used as needed to "pop" at the focals. Also, the open ceiling is articulated

with a suspended 8 ft. x 8 ft. grid system that is designed to provide a sense of intimacy over the apparel pads and unify the overall space.

**MMP: It appears that the floor fixtures, wall systems and gondolas are stock items and are used here to further the "back to basics" looks of Sears Grand. Is that the message you are delivering: good merchandise at good prices in a clean and convenient space?**
SA: The fixture system is relatively simple and timeless. At Hard lines however, a warehouse type of top rack system was introduced around the perimeter gondolas to house merchandise at higher levels (overstock) and therefore reducing the space requirements of the stockrooms.

**MMP: Is this a new concept for Sears? I must say that in many ways this store reminds me of the good, old, all-in-one department stores of my youth where you could not only furnish a home, repair and care for car and home but also dress everyone**

in the family for any occasion.
SA: This "off-mall" concept is unique to Sears, but it's also unique to the whole retail market in terms of:
• Distinctive exterior & interior environment.
• Huge merchandise assortment.
• Wide array of national brands.
• High quality of goods.

• Mass merchant prices.
It is difficult to think of another retailer that can truly claim to have all five of the above attributes under one roof.

**MMP: Again, Sherif—many thanks for your time and for sharing your insights on this project with our readers.**

# CARLOS MIELE

W. 14th St., New York, NY

Something wild, wonderful and well worth visiting opened in New York City's Chelsea District/Meat Packing area—on West 14th Street. It is the sculptured environment that has been created by the design firm, Asymptote of New York City for the noted Brazilian fashion designer Carlos Miele. To call this design "contemporary" is hardly adequate: call it amorphous, encompassing, involving —any of those words would be better to describe the cool but warm white space full of curves and cut-outs, swirling liners and luminous shadows.

According to the designers, Carlos Miele wanted the 3,500 sq. ft. space to

DESIGN: **Asymptote** New York, NY
PRINCIPALS: **Hani Rashid, Lise Anne Couture**
PROJECT ARCHITECT: **Jill Leckner**
PROJECT TEAM: **Noboru Ota, John Cleater, Peter Horner, Cathy Jones**
ASSISTANTS: **Michael Levy Bajar, Janghwan Cheon, Persa Cheung, Mary Ellen Cooper, Shinichiro**

**Himematsu, Michael Huang, Jamia Jallad, Ana Sa, Markus Schnierle, Yasmin Shahamiri**
ENGINEER: **Kam Chiu, PE, Andre Tomas Chaszer, PE**
LIGHTING: **Paul Gregory**
FABRICATOR: **555 International**, Chicago, IL
PHOTOGRAPHY: **Paul Warchol Studio**, NY
Courtesy of Carlos Miele

have an open and spacious look and he wanted the center of the store to be seen from West 14th Street as an inviting place to visit, to sit, where shopping becomes an event. And, an event it is—as well as a feast for the senses. "The architecture is a 'place' for gathering, meandering, viewing, all thought of as rituals which are set against a landscape that celebrates desire and the sensual." According to the principals of Asymptote, Hani Rashid and Lise Anne Couture, "The architectural environment is a special narrative, centered primarily on an abstracted reading of what constitutes Brazilian culture, landscape and architecture." Miele's clothes are unique, exciting and colorful and to show them off to their best advantage, the sleek, curvaceous and sculptured setting has been rendered in white with faint accents of soft green, blue and

gray. Suspended white dress forms hang from the central ceiling drop, and they are accentuated and complemented by the glowing circles on the light colored floor. Paul Gregory of Focus Lighting, who created the lighting plan for this space, embedded circular neon ring features under tempered glass in the floor and intermingled are halogen lamps. The uplighting from the floor is further enhanced by the spots set into the swelling ceiling which are targeted at the gowns on the hanging forms. Adding to the sweep of the design and responding to the effective use of the lighting is the high gloss, epoxy finished floor patterned in gray and soft green. The centerpiece of the store is the large floor-to-ceiling sculptural form that traverses the interior space. According to the designers, this "altar" element is used for both

seating and lay-down display and it was constructed of lacquer finished bent plywood over a rib and gusset substructure that was laser cut directly from CAD drawings and fabricated off site. For both the design and the fabrication of the curved forms and surfaces in the store, the designers prepared computer generated drawings and digital procedures. Some of these drawings follow this article.

The garments—hung with generous space allowances between them —fill one long wall of the space. A sinuous steel hang-rod is cantilevered off the perimeter wall to hold the hangers while below is another serpentine fixture/displayer that recalls the "altar" in the center. The dressing rooms, located at the rear of the store are also circular in design and the lighting here is quite special. In addition to the overhead illumination,

there are fluorescent lamps behind the translucent panels that form the dressing rooms. As Paul Gregory says, "The light bounces off the mirrors to create an attractive ambient glow." The storefront, like the dressing rooms, has back lit, illuminated floor and walls made of 3M diffusion film, Plexiglas and the aforementioned fluorescent lamps.

"The overall atmosphere of the space is shaped as much by the exuberant vivacity of Brazilian culture as it is by the coolness and precision afforded by new technological means of fabrication reflected in both the clothes and the architectural elements. The environment is a deliberate insertion and provocation of not only the worlds of fashion, art and architecture but also a trans-urban meditation that merges the cultures of New York and Sao Paulo."

# MAX MARA

West Broadway, Soho, New York, NY

GROUND FLOOR

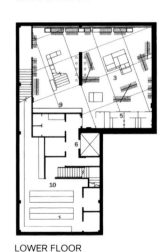

LOWER FLOOR

It all began more than 50 years ago with a "camel-colored coat and a geranium pink red suit." Max Mara, the noted designer brand, with almost 1,800 boutiques and distribution in 90 countries, was founded by Achille Maramotti, who decided to dedicate himself to the family passion: tailoring. The first collection "with its essential and exacting style, already embodied the features of the subsequent products: clean cuts and precise lines, models inspired by the brilliant French style in vogue at that time, reinvented and redesigned according to a typically Italian taste." Today, Max Mara offers a wide range of collections and numerous identities to choose from—"all based on the common foundation of quality, style and respect for the individual that this Reggio Emilia-based company consistently offers in each of its products."

What was previously a parking lot on West Broadway in trendy Soho in New York City is now a unique architectural structure of more than 6,000 square feet. It houses the Max Mara collection on two levels connected by a main staircase. There is also an elevator, as well as three other emergency stairways. The unusual, attention-getting façade is composed of a 20-degree-rotated wall covered in wood slats— "gradually separated as they gain height, with glass between." The façade includes an open window display area that includes the entrance and a closed triangular window with a glass roof. The rotation of the façade's main wall also forms a triangular skylight over the entrance that is framed in white.

According to the architect/designer, Duccio Grassi, "The volumes and spaces originated from site-related conditions, aesthetic requirements,

DESIGN: **Duccio Grassi Architects,** Reggio Emilia, Italy
**Duccio Grassi** with **Fernando Correa**
LOCAL ARCHITECT: **FZAD Architects & Design**
PHOTOGRAPHY: **Courtesy of Max Mara**

and the search for dynamic spaces and volumes based on the 20 degree grid from the perimeter axis of the lot." There are two vertical planes and two volumes and these main forms and planes are highlighted in walnut wood. One of these is the aforementioned slat wall that makes up the inward-shifted 21' 7"-high façade. The second is the T-wall that unifies the two retail levels of the shop and also creates individual retail spaces within the store. "The wood volumes enclose display and service areas, thus creating a composition of elements of different materials which play an important role in the overall composition of the project's spaces." Several skylights allow natural light to wash over the walls and "emphasize volumes and the grid from where these bi-dimensional and tri-dimensional geometries arise." The daylight also creates a constant moving pattern on the walls and merchandise while the layout of the lighting grid for this level has been incorporated within the structural elements of the composition.

There are two major retail areas on the ground level which are united by

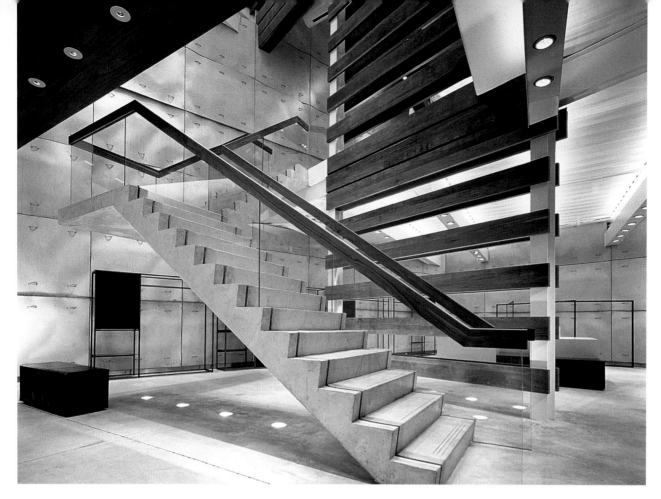

an atrium. This area is covered by a flat skylight held up from underneath by white-painted steel beams and perpendicular opaline glass ribs "that provide both shade and give structural support to the skylight." Shoppers enter under a 10-foot ceiling with recessed lighting fixtures lined up with the building's base grid, complementing the scoring lines in the poured-concrete flooring which appears throughout the shop. A "wood covered volume" on the south side of the atrium is the cash/wrap, which "seems to be held up from above and ties itself to the ground-floor slab." To the north, the second retail area is higher and made up of many sloped triangular cedar roof slabs "defined by three laminated walnut covered trusses covered up with a copper roof on the exterior." The air-conditioning ducts are exposed, painted white and extend through the open web of trusses that cross the space.

Pre-fab concrete panels appear on the north and west walls and "would seem to be sewn together to the walls with stitches of stainless steel cables."

These panels extend through the atrium and through an opening in the ground-floor slab along the north wall. "This way the light comes down the triangular skylight in the truss area and will wash down the wall all the way to the lower level, highlighting the curves in the panel's surfaces apparently made from the pressure of the stitches."

By way of the cantilevered, cast-in-place staircase—with glass and wood handrails—the shopper can go down to the lower retail level. This staircase is located in the central atrium. In the lower level, "A wood-covered wall is revealed in front and disintegrates itself in geometrical equal pieces that pop out for display purposes." The low ceiling is the exposed white-painted structural metal deck together with rotated beams that conceal the lighting for this space.

There are free-standing fixtures throughout the retail space. Some are set against the walls and are made up of natural steel cages with leather and mirror panels. These composite modules may include natural steel shelves

for display or hanging bars, while others are combinations of natural steel frames in rectangular profile tubes and shiny stainless cylindrical joists. Open and closed rectangular volumes may be arranged by these modules to form display areas. These spaces are composed of white Corian, welded natural steel sheet metal and dark brown leather for seating. Throughout the wood and concrete interior, the architects/designers used rusted and natural steel, white Corian, and walnut for furniture and finishes. The dressing rooms—on both levels—are roofless, 6'3"-high cubicles with rusted metal front partitions and white Corian interiors and floors.

In a recent list that appeared in *Women's Wear Daily*—a "bible" for the retail trade—Max Mara was listed as #1 in "Stores de Force": "high end brands with the most free-standing stores world wide." And Max Mara keeps going—and growing.

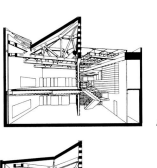

A

B

C

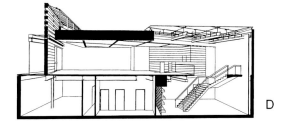

D

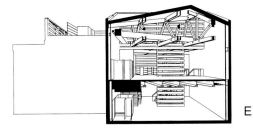

E

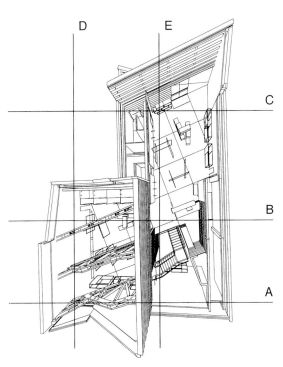

# BRUNO MAGLI

Florence, Italy

DESIGN: **CAPS,** Zurich, Switzerland
PHOTOGRAPHY: **Courtesy of CAPS**

The Bruno Magli store, as designed by Christophe Carpente, director of the CAPS architectural studio of Zurich and Paris, was conceived as "a free standing furniture concept." No walls or partitions were built in this space that is located in a handsome old building in Florence. Nor were any of the fixtures built in. "The store concept leaves open possibilities in the design of the floor layout. This gives the customer the chance to feel free to browse around and discover the products. It also allows for new arrangements of the display furniture in order to follow the evolution of the brand's strategic developments."

The new corporate identity of the Bruno Magli brand features a palette of warm gray, brown and a rich, deep brown. These colors appear in the new products, packaging, communication, and as shown on these pages, they become the color palette of the new retail design. The plastered walls behind the room frames have a marmorino-type finish in off-white and gray. The wall panels are of bleached oak veneer with copper and dark brown silk plisse fabric stretched on canvas. These are "reminders of the delicate interior upholstery of leather luggage where clothes and accessories are well protected under custom made silk pockets."

The open space is divided into more intimate spaces by means of room-sized, wooden Luoro Preto veneer frames. These create main display areas for shoes and large leather goods as well as define the ladies' and men's zones in the shop. One of the unique elements in the design—and the presentation of product—is the "wardrobe cabinet" that was inspired by a renaissance painting of St. Jerome in his study by Antonello da Messina. "This oversized cabinet in a large space creates a very exclusive area of intima-

cy." Wooden, bleached oak-type shelved containers in various sizes and proportions are piled up and positioned inside the room frame to "present the products in discreet but focused lighting. The customer is invited to enter—as into a walk-in closet at home—and select the pair of shoes or accessory that will best respond to a specific occasion or mood of the day." To create the soft, warm ambiance, a pale silk fabric covers the lampshades of the lighting fixtures that are suspended from the top of the larger room frames. In a reference to Gio Ponti's wooden equipped walls of the 1950s, accessories such as leather belts and silk items are presented inside a large Louro Preto frame on backlit, bleached oak vertical shelves—in front of an ivory leather panel with detailed stitching.

What the designer, Christophe Carpente, calls "a furniture typology for the display of accessories" is his "steamer trunk" fixture. Accessory dis-

play counters are divided into two components—like the two sides of an open steamer trunk. A bleached oak open loop, covered by a glass display bell, "embraces" a dark brown leather container—open on both ends to give access to sliding leather trays. The interior is covered with warm, red leather—"both colors represent the new corporate identity of the brand." These units are freely positioned along the path of the customer in various parts of the store. The seating arrangements in the shop, highlighted by area rugs, are arranged in front of the room frame—facing towards the products. An open, bleached oak loop is used as a display fixture and it is positioned so that it can slide along the brown leather bench that is used for seating. This puts the seated shopper in very close proximity with the featured products.

Backlit bleached oak panels start along a wall and "step over the edge of an archway" to form warm, elegant graphic signage— "indicating the path through the store." Featured products are displayed in recessed cases with translucent glass doors.

The facade of the historic building is accentuated with door handles of dark brown leather with red stitched details. The logo, in warm red, on a backlit colored Plexiglas panel set atop a brown metal plate, appears on the exterior wall between the tall, elegant arched windows. This is a design where the "details" create the whole and the end result is an elegant, finely detailed shopping environment/experience.

# YIGAL ARZOUEL

West 14th St., New York, NY

DESIGN: **Studio Dror,** New York, NY
PHOTOGRAPHY: **Dror Benshetrit,** Studio Dror

Yigal Arzouel is an exciting new star in the Fashion world and he recently opened an equally exciting, dramatic and unorthodox showroom on West 14th Street—the trendy Meat-Packing District—where he joins such other fashion luminaries such as Stella McCartney, Alexander McQueen, Carlos Miele and La Perla. The 2500 sq. ft. space is rustic and spare and—as designed by Dror Benshetrit of Studio Dror—it enhances the uniqueness of Arzouel's designs and feel for fabrics.

Arzouel's design technique is first and foremost draping and his collection "holds a natural fluidity and contouring aspect that truly enhances the female form." Dror Benshetrit, the store's designer, is a fellow Israeli and in his own work he focuses "on innovation with uses of new materials, technology and shapes and thrives on the origin of movement:"

His creations reflect a certain way of living and well being and "offer design inspiration." Thus, in this "marriage" of fashion designer with graphics and sculpture designer the result is a space filled with rich contrasts, unique materials and unusual effects. The almost gothic shop combines the rough weathered concrete floors with exposed brick walls, splintered and angled ceiling timbers, sculptural openings, floating shelves and unexpected details. Arzouel describes his fashions as "kind of unfinished and deconstructed with special stitching and trimming." He says, "I let the fabric talk to me. It tells me what to do with it." Dror Benshetrit, in a similar manner, says,

"I used the existing materials and kept it 'as is' and played with the materials." In contrast to the hard and often old materials, he added pale yellow silk curtains to create a "boudoir" feeling for the dressing rooms as well as using Terra Firma molded panels on some of the walls to add a sculptural draped fabric feel behind the suspended garments. Pegs driven into the old brick walls serve to hold additional Arzouel outfits. Like in Arzouel's garments "elements stand out in juxtaposition of strong architectural and engineered details with always devastatingly feminine and fluid fabrics."

Some of the unusual design elements added by the shop designer

include the big stone that not only serves as a coffee table but holds a mini-pool and fresh flowers—a softening touch. This rock sits in front of a retro couch of 1920s origin that serves as seating at the rear of the shop. Rough wood shelves are cantilevered off the brick wall in this rear sitting area and fragrances are displayed on them. Other pieces of antique furniture punctuate and contrast with the rustic and "crude" space.

The success of this young designer was further enhanced when he was "discovered" by the fashion stylist for "Sex and The City" and Sara Jessica Parker and Kim Cattrail were dressed in his clothes.

# BYBLOS

Moscow, Russia

"This new Byblos space is defined by continuous and decisive changes in rhythm: precise lines blending into curves then shifting rapidly to angles, encounters between reflective and opaque surfaces, the play of light and textured shadow." That is how Sean Dix, the principal designer of Dix Designs in Milan describes what he created for the Byblos boutique that opened in Moscow. The inspiration for the concept came from Dix's respect for the play of angles and curves—straight lines and arc—in the Byblos logo. Sean Dix says, "I wanted this project to recall the same kind of contrasting harmony. The other objec-

DESIGN: **DIX Design,** Milan, Italy
**Sean Dix**
PHOTOGRAPHER: **Ramak Fazel,** Milan, Italy

tive was to define the space with architecture. These are strong elements—the signature of Byblos." To create a sense of movement and define the contrasts between the curves and the straight line, Dix divided the "big, boring concrete box" into six sections with columns and arches accentuated by concealed fluorescent light strips. "The interior is framed by a decisive and rigorous geometry: a defining architecture of alternately rising and falling beams and tapering columns. These delimit this complex environment."

Located in Crocus City, Moscow, the approximately 1600 sq. ft. shop

showcases Byblos' men's, women's and accessories collections. The space is a "complex palette" of gray and white alternating—some lacquered—some opaque—some rubber and some velvet and these are accented by "an almost fluorescent dirty green and yellow." The floors are poured concrete in a rigid grid while the walls are textured with three-dimensional "waves" that have been created by using a special technique that "incises geometric patterns into composite in a computerized bas relief." The display cases seem to float as they flare out in dramatic arcs from their miniscule bases. Finished with a

special rubber coating, they provide a light-absorbing surface that "begs to be touched." The design also contrasts curves with sharp edges: "the encounter between straight and curved lines. An infinity of thin swooping ribbons of steel" make up the display tables and between the central columns of the main walls, glowing bands of light-conducting plastics serve as shelves. "The effect is that of rigorous simplicity." The clothes hangers, as designed by Sean Dix (who designed all the fixtures/fittings in the shop), have no hooks. Hidden magnets make the hangers appear inexplicably suspended from the rails of the garment display system.

For lighting there are two white chandeliers at the entrance. "Hundreds of thin, glowing arcs define the exterior of these hollow forms, creating an optical effect like vibrating bands of light." Emphasizing the geometric rhythm of the columns and beams is a gleaming ribbon of light that runs the entire perimeter of the shop.

# SALVATORE FERRAGAMO

Fifth Ave., New York, NY

"A flagship is a place for the product to come through" and Ferragamo's collection of men's and women's shoes, silk and leather accessories and ready-to-wear do "come through" in this new, award-winning, 22,000 sq. ft. showroom/salesroom designed by Janson Goldstein of New York City. Surrounded by fashionable names such as Gucci, Cartier and Saks, the space was created by combining the first two floors of two adjacent buildings on Fifth Avenue. A new facade, in two shades of imported Italian limestone, wraps around Fifth Avenue and onto East 52nd Street, connecting the two exteriors and serving "to reflect the tradition of luxury [of Ferragamo] while updating it with a contemporary elegance." Expansive double height windows permit shoppers a deep view into the interior, and narrow horizontal windows function as luxury showcases.

"The interplay between limestone and glass continues indoors where the combined spaces have their most dramatic effect; and where the architect and client's shared appreciation for material and attentiveness to detail and craftsmanship are in greatest evidence," said the designer, Mark Janson. The structural columns of the original two buildings have been concealed within a series of white partitions. "Rather than disrupt the flow of open space, they filter it to create a sequence of ultimate boutiques for ties, accessories and games, eyewear, women's ready-to-wear and a department of special order merchandise." As one enters the open and inviting spacious shop handbags—a signature Ferragamo product—are on the right. To the left is "a burst of color"—vibrant silk scarves and ties. Women's shoes are on view just beyond, on an axis with the entrance.

Contributing to the "atmosphere of classic, subdued elegance" are the white walls, limestone floors, a creamy

DESIGN: **Janson Goldstein,** LLP, New York, NY
PARTNERS: **Mark Janson, Steven Souro, Hal Goldstein**
ASSOCIATES: **Peter Weed, Takaaka Kawabata**
DESIGN TEAM: **Francesca Venturi, Leila Hadbi**
LIGHTING DESIGN: **Bill Jansing,** Dallas, TX
PHOTOGRAPHY: **Michael Weschler,** New York, NY

wool carpet, and pearlescent leather sofas—"all convey quiet warmth." Punctuating the open space are displays constructed of bright white Corian and contrasting dark walnut. Nickel silver mesh screens hang on the walls as "elegant backdrops" for the products. Suspended in the dramatic double height space is a sculptural staircase of walnut with limestone treads. It appears "to float in the space—and to anchor it." A collection of designer pillows and home furnishings are tucked beneath the staircase.

The same sense of lightness permeates the men's department on the upper level. Bleached oak floors, walnut platforms and Corian shelving anchor this space. "The sense that one is suspended over the bustle of the streetscape is reinforced by expansive windows and laminated glass partitions." The low lead content of glass renders the partitions white—"a material detail that underscores the sense of transparency." In a space at the rear of this floor is a gallery area for exhibitions including one that highlights Ferragamo's history. Others refer to contemporary art and culture.

The success of this design has led to Janson Goldstein being commissioned to design six additional Ferragamo stores.

# ALBERTA FERRETTI/PHILOSOPHY BOUTIQUE

Rue Ste. Honore, Paris, France

In the midst of the designer boutique filled Rue Ste. Honore in Paris, is the new Alberta Ferretti/Philosophy boutique. This is truly an international affair: designed in New York by David Ling Architect, fabricated in Italy and installed in Paris. It has been conceived, according to David Ling, "as a luminous theater in the city of lights."

With a limestone building and behind a two-story high glass façade, the store takes shape. "Like an open box, the interior stone and wall finishes flow outside forming the street façade." The focal architectural feature inside the store is at the center stage rear where a curved staircase takes over at the end of the long axis of the plan. The stairs are a series of floating stone steps resting on blocks of light and they are encompassed between two backlit, sandblasted acrylic planes and a recessed handrail leads the shoppers to the upper level.

The garments are housed in a soothing, elegant setting of cream-colored

DESIGN: **David Ling Architect,** New York, NY
**David Ling, Anne-Aurelie Defeche, Candy Wong, Dirk Nachtsheim**
LOCAL ARCHITECT: **Aafair**
PHOTOGRAPHY: **Guillame Guerin,** Paris, France

walls and synthetic limestone floors.
This provides "a soft background to the
minimal clarity of the two-story setting
for the collection." Accessories are art-
fully displayed in niches above the
hanging garments, on step shelves on
the second level or the rear alcoves that
are lined with floating glass accessory
shelves and a mirrored back wall—"creating the illusion of depth." Adding to
the "luminous light" ambiance are the
furniture designed by David Ling (crys-
talline glass table, sofa and chairs) and
the sandblasted acrylic shelves for the
accessories that seem to weightlessly
hover over the stone floors. The lighting plan combines backlit opaline poly-
carbonate walls, indirect lighting in the
walls and ceiling niches and the glowing shelves.

   "Alberta Ferretti's collection and
David Ling's architecture find com-
mon ground in a passion for light,
craft, translucency and layering" or as
David Ling describes his concept—
"The Incredible lightness of being."

# SEAN JOHN

Fifth Ave., New York, NY

CONCEPT DESIGN (for Sean John Co.): **Charles Soriano**
PROJECT MANAGEMENT AND ARCHITECTURAL DESIGN: **InSite Development,** New York, NY, **Gregory Anderson**
ARCHITECTURE: **TPG: The Philips Group,** New York, NY, **Ron Alalouf** and **Yabu Pushelberg,** Toronto, ON, **Anthony Simon**
PHOTOGRAPHY: **MMP/RVC**

P. Diddy has made it to Fifth Avenue! Sean "P. Diddy" Combs is a pop music icon and producer as well as the creator of a men's sportswear collection known as Sean John. The collection has been sold successfully in speciality department stores and select retailers around the world, but now the first Sean John boutique/shop has opened on Fifth Avenue opposite the tourist-destination New York Public Library.

According to Gregory Anderson of InSite Development, the designers of the 3500 sq. ft. store, "The Sean John brand crosses fashion barriers to add an upscale panache to urban influenced dress. The Sean John store, like the line, infuses its street roots with the quality of a Madison Avenue boutique to reflect the timeless style of New York, NY." The original concept for the store was inspired by pictures of "Puffy's" closets in his home. "They were organized, cozy and displayed the kind of lifestyle that Puffy wants for his customers." Thus, the store is a series of closet showcases to differentiate categories that include men's clothing, accessories, sunglasses, small leather goods, fragrance, grooming products, an exclusive line of home décor and accessories as well as a line of jewelry especially created by Jacob the Jeweler. The store is very open and inviting to the regular Sean John customer but also connects with newer ones.

The shop's new facade is clad in beige travertine with a structural steel "awning" over the door and display

windows to the left of the door. Gregory Anderson said, "We paid particular attention to the colors and material finish so as not to be intimidating to new and existing customers but still connect with upper Fifth Avenue retailers." The interior is mainly finished in ebonized South African Zebra wood, nickel metal finishes, bronze, and frosted glass walls. The floors are lightly veined travertine and the space is accented with smoky bronze acrylic and leather wall panels. Thus, the interior is mainly monochromatic: a contrast of creams, beiges and browns.

Customers enter into a "grand foyer" with a high ceiling and from there are directed down a long corridor that "echoes a fashion runway." Along the way the shopper is introduced to displayed vignettes of merchandise, "such as immaculately organized closets," that show off the different categories of prod-

uct carried in the shop. The merchandise is arranged for the shopper's perusal in "closets" spaced throughout the shop. The focal point in the store's design is the "living room": an area with oversized, overstuffed leather couches and chairs. Here shoppers can relax during the shopping experience.

Accessible through a "discreet entrance" at the rear of the shop (on E. 41 St.) is the VIP Room that boasts of a fully stocked bar and a personal shopper to assist the special visitor. Here there is oversized seating, floor-to-ceiling star fish skin wallpaper, an array of tech-toys and Puffy's favorite movies to watch on a giant screen.

Charles Soriano, VP of Retail for Sean John said, "The sleek and modern feel of the space will offer the perfect opportunity to showcase Sean John as a lifestyle brand and allow us to establish a scalable business model for planned future expansion."

# FORNARINA

Mandalay Bay Hotel/Resort, Las Vegas, NV

DESIGN: **Giorgio Borruso & Associates,** Marina Del Rey, CA
CEO: **Giorgio Borruso**
ARCHITECT OF RECORD: **Gensler Architects**
FIBERGLASS & RESIN: **T. Alongi,** Quebec
TENSILE STRUCTURES: **Eventscape,** Toronto, ON
LIGHTING CONSULTANT: **North Shore Consulting,** San Francisco, CA
PHOTOGRAPHY: **Benny Chan/Fotoworks,** Los Angeles, CA

In Las Vegas where the unusual is usual, a retail shop has opened that is truly unique. It takes one look at this fabulous environment located in the Mandalay Bay Hotel/ Resort to truly understand the meaning of the word—"unique." Giorgio Borruso, the designer of Fornarina, speaks most eloquently for his design.

"Our objective was to create, inside the chaotic bustle of Mandalay Bay and its host city, an oasis; a place of rest for the retina and the mind, a place to retire and feel comfortable. We designed a sophisticated system composed of integrated 'organs' to invite the visitor inside and expose him or her to a series of 'marvelous' products encased in clear silicon rings or displayed in unexpected floor undulations created from custom made textured vinyl containing tiny flecks of color

Upon entering this fantasy world of black and white that is bathed and saturated with rich, hot changing colored light, the eye is caught, captured and held hostage by the four giant lighting elements that hang from the ceiling in the middle of the shop. They reach the maximum height of 29 ft. and are composed of an aluminum structure wrapped in a membrane of fabric and PVC—and internally illuminated. A grid of directional lights is supported by these "tentacles."

"A mantle of vinyl, along the perimeter, rears up to become the wall and wedges underneath an outer surface. From inside the eyelid light flows down the wall to animate the product within the space," Borruso explains. This line of demarcation represents the tentative junction of two different "worlds": the floor where walking becomes an "experimental and tactile sensation," and the "sky"—sometimes "raining strange light objects, bulbs of glass suspended from fuchsia filaments or large tentacles with an obstruction of eyes which observe and at the same time indicate where to concentrate our vision, suggesting we abandon ourselves inside materials, clothes and shoes. Dressing. Changing. All in one oneiric (dream-like) experience." The flooring is Ionbead vinyl flooring and the texture suggests "walking on a bed of pearls."

Throughout, the Fornarina signature fuchsia color appears as an accent in the otherwise neutral scheme "where the product becomes the true vector of color." The design is based on creating a "visual and tactile experience and within the shop where the variety of textures and materials all enhance the experience. The design pushes consumers through the store, making sure they don't stay in one place. Walking through the store, moving and changing perspectives allow you to discover something new." Yes! There is something new and exciting and startling—and it is the new Fornarina selling environment in over-the-top Las Vegas.

# VIVA VIDA

Iguatemi Mall, Sao Paulo, Brazil

ARCHITECT/ DESIGNER: **Arthur Casas**
ASSISTANT ARCHITECT: **Juliasna Bueno Garcia**
PHOTOGRAPHY: **Tuca Reines**

Located in one of the major malls in Brazil—the Iguatemi Mall in Sao Paulo—is the newest of the Viva Vida shops. The Viva Vida chain of ready-to-wear shops is targeted at smart, stylish young women: the kind of women whose images appear in the enlarged, backlit photographs used as a decorative frieze around the perimeter wall of this new store.

As designed by Arthur Casas, the noted Brazilian designer, the space is open, light and an exquisite composition of simple geometric forms in mostly pale, neutral colors with an emphasis on native woods and leather. The high-ceilinged space has been somewhat divided by a mezzanine that overhangs a rear quarter of the main selling floor. This raised area serves as a stock room and repair space.

The designer has created a residential feeling in the open space with a "living room" in the center of the store. Here, a pair of leather-upholstered couches face each other on a carpet with small round cocktail tables in front of them. An inverted "U" shaped table of a dark native wood bisects each couch and also serves as a surface upon which merchandise can either be displayed—or outfits can be assembled. The simple, block-like forms of the couches complement the arrangement of shelves and framed insets in the perimeter walls where the stock of garments are shown.

According to Casa, the merchandise presentation simulates a well stocked and well organized "closet." The merchandise is presented face out as well as shoulder out and arranged by color in individual areas. The "closets" are divided by shelves about two feet off the ground, and additional stock—often in luggage-like containers—is stored beneath the shelves. The designer has used the white "luggage" motif decoratively as well to further the "closet" concept.

Long horizontal lines in the design counteract with the predominant vertical lines in the space. Casas has also used deep-colored wood accents throughout to underscore the play of the verticals and the horizontals. To further the residential feeling, there is a coffee machine and a small refrigerator/bar set beneath the mezzanine for the shoppers' convenience and comfort.

# BGN

Rue Bonaparte, Paris, France

The Beggon Company, located in Turkey, designs and manufactures an up-scale and fashion-aware line of women's ready-to-wear that is sold in their BGN boutiques. This new shop, on the noted Rue Bonaparte on Paris's Left Bank, is the second Parisian BGN boutique. Jean Claude Prinz of Prinz Design took advantage of the long, narrow space to create this unique-looking retail store by "playing on perspectives at the level of the ceiling" as well as cut-outs and see-throughs in the walls and the ceiling.

The façade is all glass—floor to ceiling—and the entire store appears on view from the street with the BGN logo, in black, over the entrance. The logo reappears—and just as emphatically—on the wall behind the white-on-white cube that serves as the cash/wrap

that is thrust forward into the store. The store's palette is completely neutral, with dark gray flooring and white walls and ceilings. The assorted cubes, risers, platforms and structures are covered with white Corian. Along the one long wall is a photographic mural by the Parisian photographer Caleb: a dynamic yet neutral collage of perspective lines, architectural elements and oversized figures. These murals are fixed to sliding transparent panel and can easily be changed to effect a different look in the shop.

Further back in the space s there is an architectural/sculptural element that not only forms the entrance to the changing room, but also serves as a combination seat and mirror: a seat for those who wait and a mirror for those who are

DESIGN: **Prinz Design,** Paris
**Jean Claude Prinz**
PHOTOGRAPHY: **Courtesy of Prinz Design**

trying on outfits in the curtained-off booths beyond. This decorative capricc is finished in bright red and becomes a dynamic focal element in the otherwise neutral setting.

Garments are presented both face out and shoulder out on stainless steel rods and systems provided by MCS and Vitra Shop. The floor cubes and low ramps can be used for merchandise display, seating or just as traffic barriers. The indirect lighting from below these units and from the cash/wrap add a sense of lightness to the scheme while the trenches in the ceiling and side walls also serve to provide indirect illumination to the retail space. Spotlights, directed at the product offerings, "offer a warm and welcoming brilliant spatial atmosphere."

# WHISTLES

Islington, UK

DESIGN: **Brinkworth,** London, UK
PHOTOGRAPHY: **Courtesy of Brinkworth**

The classic Whistles customer is defined as "feminine, intelligent, humorous and quirky—with a strong sense of discovery." According to Rhona Waugh, the design manager at Brinkworth—the London-based design firm—"The old store concept wasn't supporting the clothes sufficiently and we felt that there was a great scope to evolve a new concept that would support a brand with such a great reputation, both for its own label clothes and outside sourced items, to a greater advantage. What we set out to do was to create an environment that was a stronger embodiment of the Whistles spirit—using elements of the familiar and unfamiliar and juxtaposing the old and the new in a striking and refreshing way."

The new design concept was introduced in Brighton, Bluewater Mall, Wimbledon and in the Islington store which is shown here. It was also introduced as a concession boutique in Harrod's of London. In each store the design was tailored to suit the location and to "fit the opportunities and confines afforded by each space" while

using the same family of materials and ideas. The Islington store has a long, narrow plan with a bay-window shop front. By relocating the entrance, the entire left hand bay area was freed up for an arrangement of mannequins on platforms of different heights. The mannequins "face outward but also reach back into the store" and the use of the deliberately life-like poses with groups of figures loitering and posing together serves "as a reaction against rows of mannequins in formulaic neat lines." Behind the new door, in the right hand bay, merchandising units

are placed against a stunning wall of antique mirror.

Adam Brinkworth, the designer, said, "We literally chopped the space in two with a false back wall made of pink glass halfway through the store, with an almost hidden area behind it. We believe that the Whistles customer really does relish a sense of discovery and we wanted to appeal to that by countering perceived wisdom for instantly readable white-box spaces. With the front of the shop taken up by mannequins, the store effectively has three separate sec-

tions—giving it a domestic and intimate scale." A mirrored bulkhead leads to the area behind the aforementioned pink glass wall where merchandise fixtures are located beneath a timber bulkhead. In a corner is the cash/ wrap desk that is clad in antique mirrored glass as are the walls of the corridor, behind the desk, which conceal the stockroom. Opposite the stockroom are six individual changing rooms with custom nine ft. tall beveled mirrors, neon lights to the sides of the mirrors and hand made curtains for privacy.

Stained and antiqued oak flooring is used and the ceiling treatment is part high gloss aubergine (deep pur-

ple) lacquer and part wallpaper— "which continues upwards from the striking left hand wall which is both wallpapered and also partly covered by a huge scale light-box repeating the wallpaper pattern and drawing the eye in from the street." Rhona Waugh says, "We wanted to layer the new and old elements directly. Whilst the wallpaper is very traditional, the light-box over the top of it is completely modern." Brass—a rather old-fashioned material—has also been revived and used here as in the custom merchandising system which combines precision turned fittings with UV-bonded glass "so that its application is completely sleek, and a welcome

change from the stainless steel."

The overall lighting design uses simple recessed downlighters—all to highlight the two specially designed and "highly impactful" chandeliers. The smaller one (six ft. tall) is positioned over the mannequin display up front while the larger one (nine ft.) is placed over and parallel to the longer section of the light-box on the store's left hand wall. Adam Brinkworth says, "This is a store to come back to, where every visit will reveal something new. With this concept we are bringing back some of the pleasure of finding things out for yourself, without everything screaming for attention at the same time as soon as you enter a store."

# MELANIE LYNE

Sherway Gardens, Etobicoke, ON, Canada

Melanie Lyne is part of a Canadian-based company called Laura Canada and this particular branch is "an established, high end," ready-to-wear retail women's clothing operation. As with many other clothing retailers, there is a constant desire to keep updating the brand's retail image and the Ruscio Studio of Montreal was commissioned to bring Melanie Lyne into the 21st century. According to Robert Ruscio, the designer, "The only condition was that we recycle, recuperate and salvage as much of the existing elements as possible." The existing structure that was being renovated had "a lot of black granite finishes and high gloss fixtures of the early 1990s." The design team was able to "salvage" a large part of the existing ceiling, the two fitting areas located at the rear of

the store and many of the recessed standards in the walls. "The main focus was placed on up-grading the store with new finishes, display fixtures and more efficient lighting."

A more "welcoming and inviting" storefront was created by enlarging the two existing 6-ft. entrances to over 12 ft. each and completely glazing the front full height. From the storefront, the shopper can immediately see a large, oversized display table with a "casual"—but carefully selected and arrayed—show of merchandise. Added was a Barrisol skylight—directly above the table—"to help bring the viewer's attention here and give an enormous blast of light." This area actually serves as an extension of the storefront's windows. According to Ruscio, "the introduc-

DESIGN: **Ruscio Studio,** Montreal, QC, Canada
PRINCIPAL/DESIGNER: **Robert Ruscio**
PROJECT MANAGER/ASST. DESIGNER: **Yvette Casia**
PHOTOGRAPHY: **J. Michael LaFond**

tion of nesting tables into the space that typically had tall hanging racks permitted more folded garments and helped to lighten the Melanie Lyne image from a stuffy, conservative boutique into a young, stylish shopping environment."

A growing part of Melanie Lyne's business is accessories, and in this new layout they are on one side of the space and on a feature wall. "It was important for the design team to treat this part of the store like a woman's boudoir." A wall mounted stone counter—under a large wall mirror—acts as a "dresser" and the cabinets below act as on-floor storage for overstocked items. The cash back bar area—on the opposite side of the sales floor—"evokes a certain sense of

refined elegance with its clean lines and soft finishes." To bring the shoppers to the rear of the store, the designers added a giant graphic of a young woman's eye printed on a metallic vinyl wallcovering. The eyes seem to be staring at you and as Ruscio says, "It is so striking that the traffic within the store has increased dramatically."

The new interior features a vanilla white/pale beige palette that carries through from the walls to the ceiling and includes the fixtures and display props.

# VIA SETO

Carrefour Laval S/C, Laval, QC, Canada

DESIGN: **GHA Shoppingscapes,**
Montreal, QC, Canada
DESIGN TEAM: **Frank DiNiro, James Lee,
Ratiba Ayache**
PHOTOGRAPHY: **Yves Lefebvre**

This store, designed by GHA Shoppingscapes of Montreal for Via Seto, is located in the newly renovated and enlarged Carrefour Laval Shopping Center. It is a high end men's fashion boutique that features clothing that is trendy—but still elegant—and that has a new-tech look. The new store's facade is a stunning revelation and makes a strong statement in the mall. The design team at GHA (Gervais Harding Associates) took advantage of the 30 ft. height and further accentuated the positive by stressing the tall, vertical lines expressed at the opening into the store and the display windows. Limestone is combined with a "hot" new product—stainless steel mosaic—for

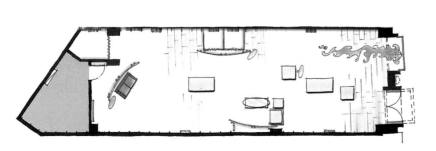

a rich, shimmering effect. The steel canopy that extends out over the double glass doors serves as a platform for a white, semi-realistic male mannequin.

Clean lines and simple, svelte, high-tech fixtures are combined with the limestone and stainless steel inside the long, narrow store as well. These materials not only suggest a crisp, masculine ambiance but they reinforce the trendy and chic of-the-moment attitude of the fashions. The floors are paved with a cool limestone that varies subtly from white to beige to gray and the exposed walls are finished in a flattering soft, beige/white color. A light—almost bleached white—wood is used with the stain-

less steel pipes on the floor fixtures, the three part counter/displayer/cash-wrap and the shelves that are cantilevered off the walls, a rich brown wood makes a strong ceiling splash along one long side of the store.

The straight lines of the space are counteracted by the two almost floor-to-ceiling curved stainless steel screens: one behind the cash-wrap and the other off centered at the rear of the store behind a contemporary couch. A third curved stainless panel with two rectangular cut-outs serves as the face of the dual dressing rooms on a side wall. An ocher colored fabric curtain, suspended from the ceiling, provides privacy and another floor length curtain of the same color

and material closes over a third changing room at the rear of the store. The simple black couch adds a touch of home to the otherwise cool environment and also invites waiting companions to rest while their friends are shopping.

In key locations in the store, floor to ceiling pressure poles stand and support dressed suit forms that show off complete outfits available at Via Seto. Throughout the space, the overhead lighting plus the special dropped light fixtures at the far end of the store and those attached to the wood ceiling panel all accent and highlight the wall displays of merchandise as well as those featured on the steel pipe and light wood tables. These

tables are set out to virtually and visually break up the long, narrow feeling of the space. The placement of these tables actually creates the traffic pattern in the store.

Via Seto won the Grand Prize for GHA for the "best new softline specialty store under 3000 sq. ft." The award was presented by the National Association of Store Fixture Manufacturers.

# SUITERS

Brookfield, WI

DESIGN: **Smart Associates,** Minneapolis, MN
PRINCIPAL: **Jim Smart**

Suiters, long a familiar men's shop in a small store in Elm Grove—a suburb of Minneapolis—moved to a space three times as large (4800 sq. ft.) in a newly constructed mall in Brookfield, WI. The shopkeepers having seen and been impressed by other stores designed by Smart Associates of Minneapolis, called upon the design firm to undertake the design of the new shop.

Jim Smart, the Principal at Smart Associates, tells about how he and his team went about solving the problems involved in this particular project.

"There were numerous challenges about working with the physical building that we were given. For one thing, it being a newly constructed building in a development, there were 'rules' that had to be adhered to regarding the exterior image of the store. Also, we had two walls of, almost, total glass and one with partial glass. This became a problem because of the amount of hanging product that had to be displayed in the store. We designed a free standing 'wall' that allowed for an exterior display on one side and hanging space on the other side. These 'walls' are designed in such a way that they can move in and out for display changes on the window side or can be relocated when it's time to give the store a fresh look.

"Another challenge was the fact that there were four entrances into the space. We designed the store in such a way that only two of the entries are used to enter the store, one is used to enter a separate business (the tailor shop, that I'll explain later) and the last door enters the stock and storage area.

"The owners had decided to set up their tailor in a separate, almost free standing, business. They are their tailors, but from the outside of the building, it seems as if they are not

affiliated. This allows for them to use the tailor shop as a separate profit center, yet have them right there as they need them.

"The target market for Suiters clothing are the upscale executives in the Milwaukee area. These clients include doctors, lawyers, etc. and they expect great service and convenient location. This new location couldn't fit the bill any better. The parking is easy and the service personnel at Suiters couldn't be better.

"To fit this image, Smart Associates Ltd. finished the store in soft, warm cherry wood tones with a few 'hits' of color on certain wall surfaces and some carpet selections. We also laid the store out so that the two entrances came into the store from the two parking sides of the store. There is a tiled central corridor running across the store at one end that connects the two entry doors with the cash wrap in the center. This produces an almost 'front door' sense coming off that corridor and into the store. There is a 'throat' running perpendicular to this corridor through the center of the store that visually connects the cash wrap to a fireplace wall at the other end

with a plasma screen television mounted above the mantel. There is a lounge area in front of the fireplace with hanging trouser bunkers lining the throat leading toward the cash wrap. On either side of the trouser bunkers we have designed a tall shirt wall with a central feature area for

displays. Fixtures play a large part of the architecture of the store, in that we used differing heights to create 'walls' like the shirtwall fixture. These help create 'rooms' within the otherwise wide open space. They also create merchandisable space at the windows, which I mentioned, by creating a wall with display on the window side and merchandising hang space on the store side.

"Each of the four dressing rooms has its own little "foyer" with a chair and lamp where a spouse can sit and wait while a fitting is going on. This fits with the owners desire for top level individualized service.

But—perhaps the biggest challenge was the incredibly tight time schedule. We did it and it worked out great."

# BARNEYS COOP

Collins Ave., Miami Beach, FL

DESIGN: **Architect of Record: RGLA, Inc.,** Chicago, IL
PRINCIPAL: **Robert G. Lyon**
PRESIDENT: **Joseph A. Geoghegan, Jr.**
VP VISUAL MARKETING & RETAIL SOLUTIONS: **Randy Sattler**
DIR. OF RETAIL PLANNING & DESIGN: **Kent Wells**
SR. DESIGNERS/CLIENT SERVICES: **Ed Hanlon, Meg Boyle**

For Barneys New York
CEO/PRESIDENT: **Howard Socol**
EXEC. VP: **David New**
VP CONSTRUCTION & FACILITIES: **Russ Delisi**
CREATIVE DIRECTOR: **Simon Doonan**
DIR. OF STORE DESIGN: **Claudia Domingues**

OUTSIDE CONCEPTUAL DESIGN CONSULTANT: **Commune,**
Los Angeles, CA
**Steven Johanknecht**
PHOTOGRAPHY: **Mark LaRosa,** Brooklyn, NY

For the design of the new prototype store for Barneys New York COOP, RGLA, Inc., of Chicago worked closely with the Barneys' in-house design team. The object was to create a unique retail environment amid the Art Deco buildings lined up on Collins Avenue in Miami Beach: one that would reinforce the COOP brand image of "Courageous, Outrageous and Contagious." This 9,000-square-foot, two story building is the first free-standing COOP to be built outside of New York City, and the designers worked to effect a memorable brand experience that would engage customers while selling the new, trend-fashions. Within the classic Art Deco white building is an ambience "filled with lavish fashion and unconventional store design elements."

Simon Doonan, Creative Director of the Barneys' New York operation said, "The mandate for this store was to make it totally memorable. With people coming from all over the globe, some with only a glancing connection with Barneys, we wanted the design to

achieve that (being memorable) by having those improbable juxtapositions we're known for." Therefore, to make the "Courageous" statement, the designers came up with new, innovative and creative ways of using such utilitarian materials as concrete and metal shelving combined with eccentric pieces. To achieve a sense of "Outrageous" flair for shoppers who are fashion-aware and daring," COOP is designed to exude a sense of excitement and a place for astute fashion customers to indulge in the industry's hottest collections," said David New, Executive VP of Creative Services. For the collections, cutting-edge designers and brands were selected, as well as COOP's private label collection, that not only cater to the local market but will speak to the Barney customer.

Recycled milk crates and antique refrigerator doors were blended with industrial elements such as aluminum floor grating systems on some of the interior walls to create a very "eco-tech" environment. The eclectic mix of thrift-shop finds and outlandish

"found" objects added to the "Contagious" feeling, which is targeted at a slightly younger than usual Barneys customer. Two of the focal walls are committed to denim. Men's denim is based on architectural, flat filing cabinets while the incorporation of the "antique" refrigerator doors on the women's denim wall creates a more retro feeling. Both areas include back storage areas as well as cash/wraps and feature back-wall collections of product with visual presentations above them. Adding a "touch of humor and sarcasm to the overall story," and the store, are the wall murals painted by Carter Kustera of New York. These appear in the dressing rooms and on

select walls in the shop. Male and female silhouettes are shown accompanied by phrases "scrawled" underneath such as "Kristen is dealing with the fact that her brother is her sister now."

"Because COOP is primed with so many unexpected surprises and fashion-forward statements, we worked very closely with fixture vendors to choose how the fixtures would be created in order to maximize merchandise capacities and create an arts & crafts, one-off, original appearance for each fixture," explained Kent Wells, RGLA's Director of Retail Planning and Design. Meanwhile, from an even more practical point of view, Randy Sattler, VP of Visual Marketing and

Retail Solutions, says, "We worked at the function of the concept with all of the Barneys COOP buying staff to ensure the design worked with all the merchandise and when executed, would move the merchandise."

In an article that appeared in *Women's Wear Daily,* Howard Socol, Barneys' CEO/President, said, "We feel that there is really nobody that has a country-wide, U.S.-based concept like COOP. It's not for every city, but it is for those cities that have a high degree of customers that are interested in fashion." Two more COOPs are planned for openings this year and the next—and then—who knows?

# CLUB MONACO

W. 57th St., New York, NY

DESIGN: **Burdifilek,** Toronto, ON, Canada
DESIGN DIRECTOR: **Diego Burdi**
MANAGING PARTNER: **Paul Filek**
SR. DESIGNER: **Jeremy Mendonca**
SR. CAD: **Tracy Margulis**
JR. CAD: **Michelle Tang**
SR. DESIGNER: **Tom Yip**

For Club Monaco
DESIGN DIRECTOR: **Heather Green**
CONSTRUCTION MANAGER: **Aldrin Alejandria**
VP STORE CONSTRUCTION: **Lorianne Glassford**

CONSULTING ARCHITECT: **NBBJ,** Seattle, WA
PHOTOGRAPHY: **Ben Rahn,** Brooklyn, NY

Located just off Fifth Avenue on the noted 57 Street is the new 5,520 square-foot Club Monaco store. This international, fashion-forward retailer has now stepped into one of the hottest retail locations in New York City. Diego Burdi, the creative partner at Burdifilek, the Toronto-based design firm responsible for this and other Club Monaco retail settings said, "The location of this store is prestigious, so without developing an entirely new concept, we played with certain elements of design and added unique features while staying within Club Monaco's distinctly modern aesthetic."

The design presents distinctive planar and linear elements throughout the design. A central vista dissects the plan of the store starting at the tall, framed front door set into the soaring two-story-high, all-glass façade. Inside, it continues back to the "image wall" —a 15-foot-high wall that not only creates a dramatic impact on the store's design, but serves as a draw to

the rear of the space. Ebony-stained jatoba flooring is used to create a sharp and dramatic contrast to the store's "white, ethereal palette." "When you look at the space, it is quite black and white—but it is very sharp." Textures, finishes and furnishings are "urban and edgy yet still classically Club Monaco modern," Burdi said. "Because we were in New York, we wanted a sense of 'wow,' and one of the things that really excited us was that the space was formerly a theater."

Highly polished chrome display cubes and dark stained walnut-veneered cubes highlight and display merchandise as well as serve to mark off areas within the shop. Merchandise is displayed in "an unintimidating manner with plenty of visual negative space that allows for clarity of merchandising and ease of shopability." Along the perimeter walls there are "wardrobe" units for the hanging and folded garments. These add

somewhat to a residential feeling and "we wanted to create the feeling of a wardrobe unit—similar to walking through your own closet." Throughout the store white headless mannequins appear in clustered groups so that "customers not only see apparel on the walls and tables, but also the theme of the merchandise."

Adding to the store's "edgy mood" are the custom brown Lucite and bronze pendant shades that provide light and focus to the cash/wrap desk, and the specially designed metal display tables and towers which are finished in a unique black wax finish with smoked shelving. In addition, such touches as simple furniture groupings ("they add value to the collection and evoke a sense of luxury"), the light ash folding tables, and the occasional area rugs all further the Club Monaco signature lifestyle. The 15-foot-high mirrored wall with concealed tri-mirror panels makes a visit

to the fitting area an added attraction and an adventure. It also adds to a satisfying shopping experience. The previously mentioned "image wall" serves as a changing art installation which contributes a sense of newness to each visit to this popular destination for the 20 to 40 crowd.

# ONLY

Odense, Denmark

Odense is Denmark's third largest city and taking up 350 square meters in the heart of that city is Only: a youth oriented fashion store. The keywords for this store are: jeans, youth, rough, loud, attitude, action, different and self-confident. The designers at Riis Retail A/S of Kolding had to make "visual" all of the above in a long, narrow space. There were three wider areas in the space and they actually ended up as "natural divisions" in the design.

The simple and open façade was reconstructed "with consideration for the original details" that were uncovered when the work began. According to Dennis Madsen, "The entrance reveals the non-inherited way of planning the shop." Mannequins appear to the right side of the entrance dressed

in the store's featured casual wear and they are backed up with a mega poster. "This area is brought top life by intelligent lighting which moves in different patterns constantly changing form and color." The lighting effects also highlight a graphic statement: "You are now on Only ground." The silver colored walls and ceiling are a unique part of this entrance area.

The desk or cash/wrap is located further inside the space—past floor racks and wall-displayed garments—and it serves many purposes. In addition to functioning as a cash/wrap it provides the DJ with an area to operate within and it is also a "hang-out place for the customers" with magazines and such—as well as accessories and cosmetics. Here too colored light

DESIGN: **Riis Retail A/S,** Kolding, Denmark
**Dennis Astrup Madsen, Lisa Nielsen**
PROJECT MANAGER: **Harold Terp**
PHOTOGRAPHY: **Jens Peter Engedal**

play on the wall behind the accessories and cosmetics "to draw as much attention as possible to this wall." The counter is curved to conform to the bend of the wall behind it which is covered with a huge graphic image. Shoppers may also "surf the Internet" on the laptops that are strapped to the poles placed in front of the wall. TV monitors are set into plexiglass boxes and are marked "Only electronics" and thus become part of the overall look of the space.

The all-important jeans area is located beyond the desk. The jeans wall consists of a series of tall rectangular framed cases in which the pants are hung face-out in two tiers. The ceiling and wall behind these cases are also bathed with changing light colors and patterns. Adding to the look of this area is the rise in the ceil-

ing where the original skylight was located. Beyond this zone is the unusual shoe wall where a giant supergraphic fills the wall and it is covered with glass panels. Glass shelves are attached to the glass wall with suction cups creating the illusion of floating shoes. "The round racks in this area state the 'rough' tone of the inventory: they are bolted between the floor and the ceiling."

A truly "different" look is the fitting room area which looks like a cube cut out of the back wall. It is covered with blue mosaic tiles and partitioned off with interior walls to look like "a public toilet or locker room. Frequently, smoke is puffed into this area that rises to the ceiling and reveals the spotlight cones. This also adds a sense of a steamy locker room."

# TE KOOP

Queen St. West, Toronto, ON, Canada

DESIGN: **II by IV Design Associates, Inc.,**
Toronto, ON, Canada
PHOTOGRAPHY: **Courtesy of II by IV**

No! This is *not* Amsterdam even though "Te Koop" (for sale) is a familiar sign on shopping streets in that water-logged city in The Netherlands. This 1,650-square-foot shop, designed by II by IV Design Associates of Toronto, is located in the up-and-coming trendy Queen Street West in Toronto. The designers were challenged to turn a typical long and narrow site into a store that reflects the "whimsical, ever-changing inventory" of colorful lifestyle accessories. The store's stock runs the gamut from hats, socks and lingerie to stuffed

toys, clocks and even a hot pink Paul Frank bicycle.

The result, shown here, is a gallery-like setting that "emphasizes the unique character of each piece of merchandise, and that is remarkably easy for the staff to manage." The strong impression begins out on the street, where the store's name is back-lit and applied over a black brick fascia. A framework or proscenium of a "mod-style, moiré pattern" in yellow and orange acrylic material—illuminated from within—creates a bright and dramatic container for the win-

dow and store entrance. Mannequins, stackable acrylic cubes and columns can be organized interchangeably in the open-sided white box (the display area up near the glass) under the pre-set lights.

On the front right entry wall is a hand-painted mural depicting a whimsical forest in graphic-novel style art. "It expresses TE Koop's paradoxical, futuristic/retro character." Standing in front of the mural are assorted height, clear Lucite cubes upon which some of the featured products are displayed. There is a

completely modular wall system of white, epoxy-coated steel panels with folded self-shelving and hanger supports. Low cabinets, below, provide on-the-floor storage as well as a top surface on which merchandise may be presented. The returns of the wall system "take advantage of any existing columns to create narrow mirrored niches that reflect and expand the merchandise display without visually interrupting the very simple layout."

An over-scaled version of these niches—painted charcoal—serves as the background for the white laminate and glass cash/wrap desk. The

assembly of colorful frosted acrylic tubes above the desk emphasize the length of the niche. A narrow, white, horizontal wall-mounted box against the dark gray wall holds a selection of "impulse-item toys." Square and curved white plinths of assorted heights are arranged down the center of the narrow store "to support the highly flexible inventory." Some have glass cases on top and some—with the addition of pillows—become seats. The black, white and charcoal color palette of the walls, ceiling and floor continues here to further highlight the merchandise.

A white partition—at the rear of the store—not only marks off the changing room area but also serves as a giant screen upon which contemporary animated films are projected. "This novel approach to the traditional 'back wall feature' displays spirit—not merchandise." A great attraction of light and motion that can be seen from the entrance and even on the street, it is a real draw into the store and to the rear of the retail space.

# DANIER LEATHER

Yorkdale Shopping Centre, Toronto, ON, Canada

Last year we introduced the handsome Danier Leather shop, designed by Burdifilek of Toronto. The design won several top design awards. However, in keeping with the retailer's strategy to "re-style the brand across North America," they commissioned Burdifilek to create a new roll-out concept based on the original shop design. This new roll-out design debuted in the Yorkdale Shopping Centre in Toronto. According to the designers, "The sleek new design is a spin-off from the flagship store and includes new custom finishes that complement Danier's new modern leather merchandise and fashion designs."

Similar to the original design are the custom display cubes fitted with sandblasted acrylic trays, the leather slat

DESIGN: **Burdifilek,** Toronto, ON, Canda.
**Diego Burdi, Tom Yip, Jeremy Mendonca,**
**Tracy Morgulis, Mauro Lobo-Pires, Indrajit Motalka**

wall, and the bold-colored panels. "We were able to play with finishes, veneers and textures to come up with cost-effective translations of the costlier design elements we custom designed specifically for the flagship—elements are similar, but they evoke a slightly different feeling," said Diego Burdi, the creative director of the design firm.

Creating the feeling of a shop-within-a-shop—up front—are the sleek metal shelf frames over the low-slung handbag and accessories display platforms. The color and material palette for the roll-out concept includes pewter color stained, quarter-cut, cracked ashwood on the display furniture and columns; exposed antique bronze metal work and hand stitched leather details. Together they set Danier apart in "a unique characteristic manner and provide a memorable physical relation to the brand."

# TANNER KROLLE

Sloane St., Knightsbridge, London, UK

DESIGN: **Caulder Moore,** Kew, London
**Ian Caulder, Penelope Ward, Dione Fague**
PROJECT MANAGER: **Rory Harte**
SHOPFITTERS: **Umdasch Shop Concept, GmbH**
GRAPHGIC DESIGN: **Katie, Tilleke Exposure**
PHOTOGRAPHY: **Media Wisdom, Giles Christopher**

Where Sloane Street meets Basil Street —just a few steps from Harvey Nichols and the Knightsbridge tube station, is the new, small but sparkling Tanner Krolle leather goods shop. In just a few short months the corner has been dubbed Tanner Krolle corner and much of the shop's success is due to the stunning illusions created by Caulder Moore design firm and the striking, even if sometimes invisible, fixture systems by Umdasch.

The challenge, according to Ian Caulder of the design firm, was "to create a space that functions as a transient and dynamic gallery area, delivering a modern, ever-changing backdrop to the mouth-watering collection of sexy and irresistible handbags and luxury leather accessories." The store design has a technical, industrial and yet very sexy vibe as it features glass, concrete and silver "offering a juxtaposition of styles, hard

against soft, feminine meets masculine, contemporary against heritage." Backwashes of color animate the translucent white glass walls against which the Tanner Krolle bags are suspended. Above the floating displays white glass transforms to opal frosted glass upon which are cast projections of images, graphics and pieces of film. "The appeal is one of an art installation—a moving image gallery and luxurious, alluring, retail store."

The white tile floors and white glass walls with the clear glass cantilevered shelves give way on the right to an almost non-existent glass staircase that leads to the lower level of the shop. Glowing red stripes on the treads indicate where the steps are even though the staircase is re-imaged in the mirrored wall beside it. On the lower level the same whiteness suggests a larger space and here, too, light images appear on the white floor tiles and on

the frosted, backlit perimeter walls.

Guy Salter, Chief Executive for Tanner Kroll said, "Some store designs get in the way of the product. At Tanner Krolle we believe our bags must be the hero, so we wanted a flexible but beautiful backdrop that could change with the seasons. We also wanted a fun, dynamic and accessible environment for our customers to shop in." The high tech nature of the design combined with the use of imagery and color deliver a flexible contemporary environment within two ancient London buildings. And as Tanner Krolle would agree—"no overweening retail design gets in the way when you have bags as beautiful as ours." Continuing to push boundaries of luxurious style and innovation, Tanner Krolle, remains true to its 150 years of London-based heritage with this store.

# SCHEDONI

Coral Gables, FL

Schedoni stands for hand crafted specialty leather goods and accessories and the challenge for the Pavlik Design Team of Ft. Lauderdale, FL, in designing this retail environment was to introduce the retailer as "a couture destination and as a fashion leader in the luxury leather goods industry." By creating an engaging and contemporary design, the ambiance complements the timeless fashion of the merchandise and the unique "minimalist" setting "reflects an exclusive lifestyle."

The store's interior is a cool white and beige except for the far end wall which has been painted a fiery Ferrari red color. This bright focal element, which also optically brings the back end of the store up closer to the entering shopper, is also a signature since it subtly reminds the upscale,

luxury item shopper that this leather retailer is also the producer of the custom leather products used in Ferrari autos. "Chic" and "Minimalist" best describe the sharp, clean lines of the interior and the architectural elements create a simple but dramatic setting for the merchandise display. There is a sense of dynamic energy in the design which is created by the use of intersecting planes of the ceiling liners, the floors and the walls.

While porcelain tiles cover most of the floor there are three squares of pale beige carpeting that make a geometric pattern on the floor and they also offset the geometry of the design. A long, warm, white, laminate-covered display table angles off kilter—from the entrance towards the rear of the shop—and unique pendant lamps drop from the ceiling above it to

DESIGN: **Pavlik Design Team,** Ft. Lauderdale, FL
PRESIDENT/CEO: **R.J. Pavlik**
DESIGN ADMINISTRATION DIRECTOR: **Placido Herrera**
CREATIVE DIRECTOR: **Sherif Ayad**
PROJECT DESIGNER: **Troy Griffin**
PROJECT MANAGER: **Dalit Dray**
LIGHTING DESIGNER: **Amy Ann Straley**
PHOTOGRAPHY: **Dana Hoff, Dana Hoff Photography,** Lake Park, FL

highlight the product display. The table follows the canter/skewed angle of the wall behind it which, at the same time, angles the merchandise presentation towards the entrance for optimal viewing from outside the store. The opposite wall features built-in display shelves which are also self-illuminated.

The red focal wall is also off-centered with floating shelves to one side and the cash-wrap/showcase set in front of it on the other side. Seating is provided around one of the laminated cubes which is capped with an internally lit rectangle. Saddle leather pillows cover the shelf-like seat projections from the cube. This allows the shopper to sit while her package is being prepared for her.

Up front, the low built-up platform under the window and extending along the entrance wall serves as

the window display area. Within the nine niches on the wall adjacent to the window are close up, detailed photos to "introduce the customer to the refined quality and details of Schedoni." Throughout, the "hierarchy of the luminous high ceiling planes create a voluminous space," and the lighting contained within the ceiling affects an overall warm and welcoming ambiance within the shop.

Schedoni and the Pavlik Design Team won the award for "outstanding merit in design of a soft goods store under 3,000 sq. ft." from the NASFM.

# STEVE MADDEN

West 34th St., New York, NY

DESIGN: **DZO Architecture,** New York, NY
**David Sereo, Elena Fernandez**
AND
**Future Pace Design,** New York, NY
**Manfred St. Julien, Diego Rosales**
CLIENT: **Steve Madden LTD**
EXEC. VP: **Marck Jankowski**
DIR. OF STORE CONSTRUCTION: **Dana Yanniello**
PHOTOGRAPHY: **Bilyana Dimitrova**

Joining the excitement of the "horizontal mall" that stretches along West 34th Street from Fifth Avenue over to Seventh Avenue in New York City is the new and completely redesigned Steve Madden store. In keeping with the company's ongoing focus "on the fresh and vibrant tastes of the teenage market," the renovation was accomplished through the collaborative efforts of DZO Architecture and Future Pace Design, both of New York. Working closely with the client, the result is a bright, fresh look that blends the original industrial look of the Steve Madden stores with soft curves of concrete and metal mesh plus an effective graphic wall display. According to David Sereo, a principal at DZO Architecture, "We wanted to blend industrial strength materials with soft curves and materials to create this lounge feeling."

The red carpets help to delineate

sitting areas while the poured concrete floor carries the heavy traffic through the 1800 square foot store. The floor is highlighted with poured concrete tables complemented by the red latex upholstery. The elliptical tables are cast in wax concrete and shoppers can approach these feature displayers from any direction. They also help to establish traffic patterns on the floor. In addition to a distinct space set aside for men in what is predominantly a women's shoe store, there is also a section for the introduction of jeans and tees—a new clothing area for Steve Madden.

New styles of shoes are featured on the long display wall. A long, stainless steel perforated surface, backed up by a mirror, is folded to provide display platforms for the shoes. The multiple layers of mesh blend to create "a moiré effect with the reflecting customer's silhouettes." The shoes are backlit and seem to float in space. The "feature" wall is a system of modular, diamond-shaped lighting panels and product support. The layout and arrangement of these elements can be modified according to seasonal or collection changes. Shoes as well as accessories and apparel can be displayed on this brushed steel configuration. Hang rods and shelves are combined on this wall along with panels of blue glass that attach to the light panels used to highlight the special garments.

Special events and promotions are held in the lounge area at the rear of the long, narrow store. These are centered around trilobed seating/display units. The seating encircles a bronze semi-transparent coiled mesh screen that, in turn, surrounds mannequins in the new jean collection. By word of mouth, by the traffic through the store, and by the sales, the new design is attracting the shoppers it was designed for.

# GORDON SCOTT

New St., Birmingham, UK

DESIGN: **Dalziel + Pow,** London, UK
**John Scott, Martin Letts**
PHOTOGRAPHY: **Nathan Willock**

Birmingham seems to be busting out all over as a new, trendy, fashion-oriented area in the UK. With its new Selfridges, Harvey Nichols and other noteworthy stores opening up, it has become the place where the action is. For Gordon Scott, a traditional footwear retailer, this new design by Dalziel + Pow of London opens new opportunities in a new location. John Scott, one of the designers, said, "The new store is a rich combination of traditional materials and a confident approach to the planning and detailing of furniture. The design of

display cabinets, tiered tables and bespoke leather chairs create a kind of 'contemporary-traditional' look which gives the brand a broad appeal."

This store appears on the main shopping street and adds to the "rejuvenation" of that street. Since the Bullring was built and developed, many retailers have moved there and thus one of the vacancies made this space available for Gordon Scott. The façade reflects the look and feel of the period architecture on New Street but the open windows allow shoppers to see into the light, neutral-colored

space. While the custom printed wallpaper carries the company's logo and the softly-illuminated fabric drapes "help to create a more feminine mood," it is the deep, dark stained wood wall cabinets against the light walls and the deep brown leather chairs that pop out of the design. Back painted panels, on the cabinets "provide a rich backdrop for the stock." In the Men's area the panels are painted a deep "petrol blue" and a rich plum color takes over in the Women's area. Polished chrome display tables and bases on the leather chairs "create a sharper edge to the identity." A tasteful collage of prints in assorted sizes and colored frames appears up front over the floating glass shelves—adding a residential quality top the design. That same feeling is further enhanced by

the suspended fabric shaded lights that drop from the ceiling that is also filled with recessed incandescent lamps and the illuminated draperies on the walls. The cash/wrap counter continues the dark wood detailing and it serves to separate the men's area from the women's.

"The environment responds to this (the classic brands) by offering a level of luxury and quality that supports these brands without portraying an overtly exclusive image." Though this store has "created a stir" in Birmingham, future plans for a rollout of this pilot store will depend upon its success on New Street.

# SKECHERS

Times Square, New York, NY

DESIGN: **ME Productions,** Marina Del Rey, CA
PRINCIPAL DESIGNER: **Michael Eschger**
PROJECT MANAGER/DESIGNER: **Emilio Verduga**
ARCHITECT: **David Ketch**

ARCHITECT OF RECORD: **Coggan & Crawford,** Brooklyn, NY
LIGHTING DESIGN: **Lighting Design Alliance,**
Long Beach, CA
SENIOR DESIGNER: **Archit Jain**
DESIGNER: **C. Lindsey Perkins**

PHOTOGRAPHY: **Jay Rosenblatt**

The excitement—the color—lights and flair that have made Skechers stores a magnate for teens 'n' twenties throughout the U.S. and Europe has reached a new peak—a new height of pizzazz—in the 6,400-square-foot Times Square store that opened with all the hoopla of a Hollywood premier. Michael Greenberg, President of Skechers, speaks of this new flagship store's location as "a challenging retail environment" since Times Square—like other parts of New York City visited in this edition—resembles an outdoor mall rather than the theatrical district it has always been. For this store—for this location—and for the competition that abounds and surrounds, the designers at ME Productions, under Michael Eschger, who has developed the Skechers retail brand image for years, were told to "push the boundaries."

Speaking for the design firm, Emilio Verdugo said, "Times Square is definitely the crown jewel in Skechers roster today." It is "the most elaborate and detailed of any of the nearly 120 stores" that ME Productions has designed for that retailer. The backlit, translucent blue panels that have become a Skechers signature element once again sets the look and the theme. Twenty-five feet off the ground is a dramatic, dome-shaped fabric canopy—circled and segmented with rows of lights. It suggests a circular space below. That feeling is enhanced by the angled, glowing panels that carry a full display of shoes. They seem to "curve" with the dome above. Behind the cash/wrap, that becomes a sort of divider in the space, is a dark and intimate area: the Groove Lounge. Equipped with seating, plasma screens, listening stations and a bar, this is a popular meeting place in Skechers. Glass mosaic tiles in shades and tints of blue become the back wall of the Water Bar and the tiles are enhanced by the steady flow of water running down the wall accented by beams of light from MR16 bulbs installed in the ceiling. The 13-foot counter, previously mentioned, is accentuated by the changing colors of lights and the pair of pedestals—one at either end—also highlighted by the varying colored lights playing behind the translucent

covering. Light is a most important element in the design. It sets the look of the blue panels around the perimeter walls, the domed ceiling design, and the subtle glow of the Groove Lounge. Wood floors, glass mosaic tiles, vinyl upholstered benches and seats, and stainless steel-wrapped elliptical display tables on the floor highlighted with glowing translucent plastic shapes, are all part of the look of this Skechers. Between the blue panels and the raised ceiling are backlit, lifestyle-colored graphics and three giant plasma screens, set in front of the lounge, that all help to create the desired ambiance and set the mood for the shoppers.

Not only is this Skechers the "crown jewel," it is also a brilliant, shimmering and most welcome addition to the blaze of light and color that is Broadway and Times Square. And—Skechers holds its own even in the midst of All That Jazz.

# QUIKSILVER

Times Square, New York, NY

DESIGNER: **Steven Sclaroff Design,** New York, NY
**Steven Sclaroff**
ARCHITECT OF RECORD: **TPG,** New York, NY
LIGHTING DESIGN: **Johnson Schwinghammer**

for Quiksilver:
SR. VP OF RETAIL: **Gregg Solomon**
VP OF VISUALS: **Steven Jones**

PHOTOGRAPHY: **Michael Vitti**

Surfing on the Square—Times Square? Who would have thought it: a surfboarding/youth-oriented/beach-party lifestyle store on Times Square in the center of New York City's thriving, throbbing and be-bopping theater/tourist district? Well, it is there and it is making a bold,

colorful stand with its sweeping front and three giant wavy LED screens upon which surfing images are projected in vivid color. There is enough color, light and pizzazz at Quiksilver for it to hold its own in the midst of the sound and fury of W. 42nd St.—probably the most populated and

trafficked corner in New York.

It seems that the recent influx of movies, reality TV shows, and fashion trends have propelled surfing, beachwear and things Hawaiian into the mainstream urban sensibility. According to Steven Jones, VP of Visuals for Quiksilver, the Hunting-

ton Beach, CA company that is making the big splash with this 3,000 sq. ft. store, "All that surf exposure—the good and the bad—is all positive for the brand. It helps raise the awareness of surfing as a whole and brings it more into popular culture." Gregg Solomon, Sr. VP of Retail for the company said, "It's kind of a west coast, casual, outdoor, beach lifestyle that is a more aspirational customer base than actual surfers."

There is no mistaking the "surf-boarding" theme in this store as designed by Steven Sclaroff of Steven Sclaroff Designs, New York, who worked closely with Steven Jones and others at Quiksilver. "I showed images of things that I thought evoked board sports and ultimately the walls were clad in curved planes of plywood—meant to look like skateboard ramps. There is a video 'scoop' in the center of the store that looks pretty much like a wave with its projecting surfing images." Fifty full-size surfboards hang down from the high ceiling to further carry through the surf/beach theme. Sclaroff was inspired to use the boards this way because the basis of his design concept was the surf board stores back in the 1960s—out on the West Coast —where the boards seem to overwhelm and overflow from the shack spaces. He also feels that the ceiling treatment carries through the movement generated by the wave-like wall of monitors. This wall is the focal element in the design and is visible from out in the street. The 20 ft. video "wave" is comprised of 63 screens. It not only creates a dramatic statement behind the cash/wrap counter but it solved the problem of accommodating an odd shaped wall that backs up the entrance to the subway behind it. The hanging surfboards also serve as lighting fixtures since fluorescent lamps are attached to the upper side and light up the ceiling as well as provide the store's ambient light.

For the flooring Hawaiian pebbles were used to advance the beach concept and the projected sunny images along with the theatrical lighting fixtures create a sun-filled space. "We wanted it to be bright since all the board sports take place outside, in the sun," says Sclaroff. The floor fixtures were constructed of white MDF and fiberglass plywood: a mix of unfinished against a slick white lacquered finish.

Though the design is not actually a prototype for future Quiksilver stores — it is more like a flagship store — many of the concepts and details envisioned by Sclaroff will be appearing in future company stores. Though surf boarding is the name of the game and the theme of the store, the merchandise does appeal to non-surfers as well. According to Sclaroff, "Somehow I think the casual character of the clothing and the feel of sport and enjoyment are universal and appealing in a friendly, relaxing way." From the crowds that fill the store day into night, the appeal is definitely working.

# ADIDAS

Siam Discovery Center, Bangkok, Thailand

Bob Neville, head of Creative Services for Adidas in the Asia/Pacific region, worked with Rkurt Durrant of RKD Retail—a Bangkok-based design firm —to create the prototype that would be an Asia-Pacific "response to the programs that were developed by Adidas in Europe and North America." This new 1,400-square-foot store is in the Siam Discovery Center in Bangkok.

The concept effectively integrates changing graphic images with adaptable, flexible and interchangeable wall-system units. The almost-all-white space is accented with the signature Adidas aqua/blue color and monochromatic graphics in the same cool color. Brushed stainless steel is the other accent. Simple, roll-about H-racks on heavy casters carry the shirts while white laminate-covered shelves, on these same units, hold the accessories. The curved front panel of the rack is finished with an exchangeable graphic collage that highlights a particular sports activity. Gym equipment provided the inspiration for the brown, leather-like tables that also show off featured products up front.

Of special interest is the shoe wall at the rear of the space. Almost 120 Adidas shoe styles are presented on small, white, cantilevered shelves that reach out from rectangular panels with rounded tops and bottoms.

DESIGN: **RKD Retail/IQ**
PRINCIPAL: **Rkurt Durrant**
SR. CREATIVE DIRECTOR: **Elle Chaiyakul**
JOB CAPTAIN: **Paophan Poomnoi**
PHOTOGRAPHY: **Pruk Dejkhamhaeng**

These panels are mounted on brushed
steel uprights and the shoes are highlighted by the spots set in the fascia
board over this area.

The other wall systems carry the
identifying signage on top with various sports listed. The wall system can
accept panels, shelves, hang-rails,
face-outs or feature waterfalls. The
partial wall, on the left side of the
store and visible through the glass
façade, best shows how effectively the
store has been visually merchandised.
The lighting throughout, a mixture
of incandescent spots and fluores-
cents in the ceiling troughs, flood the
space with a bright, light but cool
ambient look.

# SYNOPTIK

Ostergade, Copenhagen, Denmark

DESIGN: **Confect,** Kolding, Denmark
PHOTOGRAPHY: **Courtesy of Confect**

Anybody who wears glasses and lives in Denmark, Sweden, Norway or Northern Germany knows that Synoptik is synonymous with fashionable eyewear. The design, shown here by Confect of Kolding, is the first of the new look for the company and it has been implemented in the heart of Copenhagen.

The basic premise was to create an arrangement where the customer and the product presentation "are in focus." To achieve that "focusing," the designers of Confect came up with the concept of different "rooms"—or a

variety of areas or boutiques within the store in which the shopper may "satisfy a variety of customer experiences." Instead of the frames being shown on the walls, they are now moved out to the floor and shown on polished aluminum modules suspended from the ceiling. Also, "all glasses have been given individual shelf space to promote the product and hence make it more visible to the shopper." These shelves are made of polished gray steel and finished off with soft, natural rubber pads. Throughout, the design team has maintained a soft, neutral palette of grays and whites: dark gray carpets, light teak woods and rubber tiles for flooring and frosted acrylic wall panels illuminated from behind. The walls are now used for graphic promotions, posters and special product displays in flush showcases.

There are some specialty boutiques in the new concept. In the Trend area men and women can find the newest and hottest looks in eyeglass frames and sun glasses. They are also shown

suspended from the ceiling on these polished aluminum modules with a central core of opal acrylic tubes. A Child's area looks and feels like a playground but the eyeglass frames are visible in the dark blue rotunda that features indirect lighting. There is also a Café that doubles as the waiting area. Here the designers used teak flooring with medoc colored walls. The all-important counter, made of white ash, has been divided into a series of serve areas "to create a more personal and intimate atmosphere." The walls behind the counter are painted ultra violet.

The new concept, according to Torben Rath Hansen, the Managing Director of Synoptik, gives "Synoptik a more modern design and our customers a more complete shopping experience in the store."

# CASA & IDEAS

Parque Arauco Mall, Santiago, Chile

DESIGN: **Space Planning International,** Santiago, Chile
CEO: **Ricardo Rocha**
DESIGNER: **Sofia Pereya**
ARCHITECT: **Gabriel de Rosas**
DESIGN ASSISTANT: **Denise Batiste**

LIGHTING: **Oriana Ponzini**
PHOTOGRAPHY: **JE**

The Parque Arauco Mall, located in a suburb of Santiago is a shopping destination and the new Casa & Ideas store with 18,000+ sq. ft. is now part of the mall's attraction. This vast expanse with ceilings at $13^1/_2$ ft. is filled with many categories of home furnishing items and home gifts as well. According to the designers, the layout was "created with the intention, of optimizing and maximizing the use of the space and establishing numerous focal points along the racetrack circular plan."

To accomplish the desired effect, perimeter areas and islands of merchandise were established—"to facili-

tate the movement of the visitor through the store in a guided fashion." The flooring colors and patterns and the lighting plan were also designed to enhance the shoppers' circulation in the space. In addition the designers felt the need—in this large space—to create smaller, more intimate, more home-like spaces. To accomplish this, they relied on the use of natural materials such as pine wood and vegetable dyes.

Considering the volume of items carried in the store, the space has been organized and set up to make finding the right item both simple and pleasant. In addition to the over-

head directional and departmental signage to start the shopper off in the right direction, there are many clever and well coordinated focal displays along the way to side-track the shopper and offer impulse items to add to the shopping basket. Space Planning International has done a brilliant job of color-coordinating the multitude of product offerings and assembling them in easy to see, easy to select and easy to coordinate clusters. By varying the ceiling heights throughout, "the idea of movement was introduced and these variations also help to accentuate the focal display points in the space." Using a mostly neutral color scheme of light colors accented with natural woods along with simple geometric forms, and by dividing the space into specific areas or departments as can be seen by the floor plan, Casa & Ideas is a satisfying and fun place to shop.

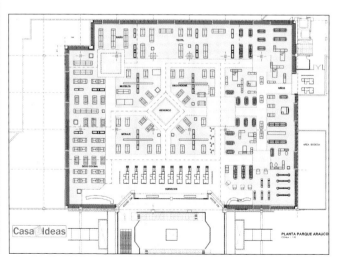

# TELUS MOBILITY

Montreal, QC, Canada

Recognizing the need to maintain their predecessor's (Clearnets) "future friendly" image and to re-launch the Telus brand, the company called upon Burdifilek of Toronto to redesign and evolve their existing retail store design concept. This, the flagship store on Ste. Catherine Street in Montreal, now stands out from the competition in a unique, historic building. According to the designers, the juxtaposition of "nature meets technology" is literally reflected in the design. Elaborate vaulted and coffered ceilings, cornices and moldings serve as an

"antique envelope" for the clean, contemporary finishes and custom fixtures. And—all of this is set out in a "simplistically simple" floor plan.

Situated around the almost all-white environment are spacious, easy-to-find, easy-to-shop bays. Shown in these areas around the perimeter wall are displays of cellular phones and accessories. Set out on the floor—under the coffered ceiling that carries long lines of spots—are purple and white plastic pedestals with museum-type cases on top in which the featured products are displayed. Simple, square

DESIGN: **Burdifilek,** Toronto, ON, Canada
DESIGN TEAM: **Diego Burdi,
Paul Filek, Tom Yip,
Mariko Nakagawa, Maura Lobo-Peres**

tube frames—attached to the floor and the ceiling—carry the message signs, sample phones to handle and boxed phones ready to go. In all this whiteness there is a sharp yellow-green color of frosted Lucite that appears and reappears as a bright and lively accent.

A centrally placed internet kiosk encourages shoppers to interact with each other and familiarize themselves with Telus' numerous web-ready functions. At the very rear of the sales area is an 11 ft. x 15 ft. glass wall featuring a giant translucent image of a violet colored

dahlia—the traditional blossom in the signature color. Behind this partition is an enlarged customer service area furnished with classic Saarinen chairs and pedestal tables. It is here in a "casual and soothing" environment that customers can enquire about their Telus accounts.

"Understated yet functional fixturing systems, spun aluminum light fixtures, brushed stainless steel and milky Corian surfaces complement Telus' trademark purple color, and further maintain the customers attention to the products and strong visuals."

# I-MODE

The Hague, The Netherlands

DESIGN: **fca! Retail,** Amsterdam
DESIGN TEAM: **Stephan Pangratz** with **Alexai Drozdov** and **Rene van Rijk**
STRATEGY TEAM: **Ron Cijs** with **Nico de Jong**
PROJECT MANASGER FOR KPN MOBILE: **Ms. Tijntje Louwers**
PHOTOGRAPHY: **Courtesy of fca! Retail**

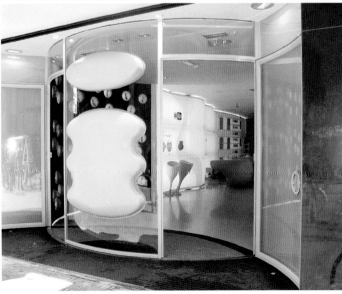

KPN Mobile is one of the leading mobile phone operators in Europe. KPN asked fca! Retail to create and design a store concept to bring to life the world of I-mode and to enable consumers to experience the world of I-mode. Working closely in association with the client, the designers created this new and exciting showroom/salesroom that was introduced in Japan, Germany and this installation in The Hague.

The virtual world of I-mode had to be transformed tò a unique, physical, three-dimensional experience. In an interactive way the I-mode store has become a guide to all

Het kan echt

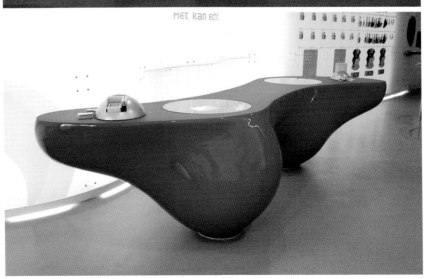

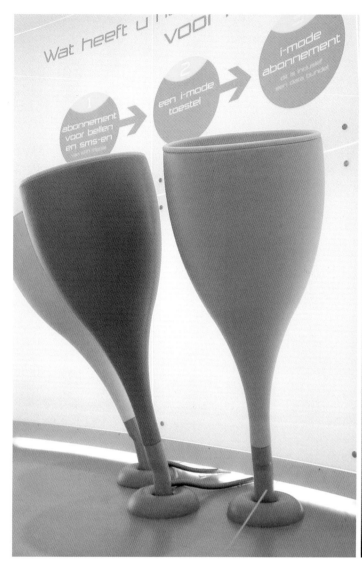

aspects of I-mode. Everything has its own place in the store: services, hardware, content providers and personal applications. The space is divided into three spacial zones. The "Confrontation Zone" is the entrance with the brand icon for I-mode and just beyond is the "Information & Content Zone" which is "the hearth of the store." Here, all information about how to purchase I-mode and its services are centralized. The "Content Forest" consists of 14 curved metal poles of approximately nine feet in length and on these poles the various content providers are displayed and "explain their content virtually and interactively." The red check-out station is a "work of art" in its amorphous and sinuous form of almost 13 ft. in length. At the rear

of the store is the "Experience Zone." There is a huge area with a rounded back wall (36 ft. x 9 ft.) upon which moving images are projected. "This symbolizes the uniqueness of I-mode: with I-mode you have the world in your back pocket." Shoppers are invited to sit on the bright, colorful plastic "sitting rocks" and activate a pop-up screen to build their own I-mode sites. "This is where the world of I-mode enters the store larger than life."

The I-mode hand sets are on display in a sound square of two purple walls which contain over 100 spheres in which the hand sets are visible. By touching some of these spheres, the visitor activates new and trendy ring tones. On the green tinted lucite panels—the "Grasslands"—the assorted accessories are shown on

green pegs that extend through openings in the panels.

According to Stephan Pangratz, creative director of fca! Retail, "Fluid forms and organic shapes, combined with bright primary colors are the main style elements of the shop. This design was inspired by nature, for example the 'Content Forest,' 'sitting rocks,' 'large tulips' and 'grassfields.' The translation of these metaphors into store design results in a futuristic look and enhances the theme of the shop: virtuality becomes reality."

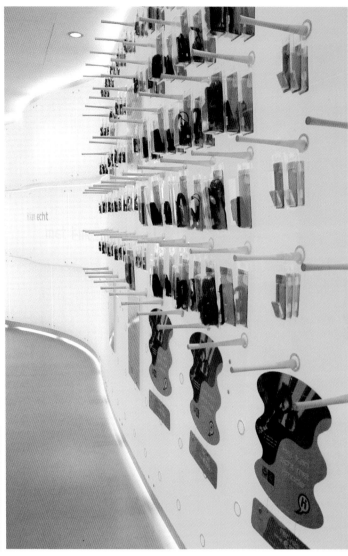

# globalshop

March 26-28, 2006 • Orlando, FL
Orange County Convention Center

www.globalshop.org

GlobalShop 2006 is the largest store design and in-store marketing show that showcases the industry's leading and most cutting-edge exhibitors.